PEPPERS
of the
WORLD
An Identification Guide

PEPPERS
of the
WORLD
An Identification Guide

by Dave DeWitt and
Paul W. Bosland

Ten Speed Press
Berkeley, California

Ten Speed Press
Post Office Box 7123
Berkeley, California 94707

Distributed in Australia by E. J. Dwyer Pty. Ltd., in Canada by Publishers Group West,
in New Zealand by Tandem Press, in South Africa by Real Books, and in the United
Kingdom and Europe by Airlift Books.

Cover and book design by Catherine Jacobes

Library of Congress Cataloging-in-Publication Data
DeWitt, Dave
    Peppers of the world: an identification guide/by Dave DeWitt and Paul W. Bosland
        p.   cm.
    Includes bibliographical references (p.) and index.
    ISBN 0-89815-840-0
    1. Peppers—Identification. 2. Peppers—Pictorial works.
I. Bosland, Paul W. II. Title
QK495.S7D48 1997
633.8'4—dc20   96—15364
                                   CIP

First printing, 1996
Printed in China

1 2 3 4 5 6 7 8 9 10—00 99 98 97 96

CONTENTS

Dried peppers for sale in Guatemalan marketplace

ACKNOWLEDGMENTS

Thanks to all the pepper-lovers who helped with this project:

Alton Bailey
Chel Beeson
Judy, Willie, and Emily Bosland
LeRoy Daugherty
Ed and Jan Eckhoff
Victor Espinosa
Jeff and Nancy Gerlach
Max Gonzalez
Charlie Hawkins
Antonio Heras-Duran
Jaime Iglesias
Robert Jarret

Gil Lovell
José Marmolejo
The NMSU Chile Team
John Owens
Rich Phillips
Richard Rice
Richard Sterling
Sharon Trujillo
Javier Vargas
Steve Vicen
Eric Votava
Mary Jane Wilan

▲▲▲▲▲▲▲

Stringing paprika in Hungary

▼▼▼▼▼▼▼

INTRODUCTION

THIS GUIDE IS THE RESULT OF four years of growing and pho-
tographing peppers from all over the world. Although it contains
color field photographs of hundreds of varieties, it was impossible to
include all the varieties in the world—that would require a truly mas-
sive volume. Based on the numbers we grew to cull the final selections
down to what is published here, and considering the USDA collection
that we utilized as a main seed source, we estimate the total number
of world varieties to be between two and three thousand. Even this
estimate is highly speculative, considering the propensity of the *Capsicum* genus to cross-pollinate.

Thus this book can only be a sampling of the world of peppers,
so we apologize in advance if your pet pepper isn't included, or if you
can't find a picture for a cultivar name you have. Although there are
thousands of pepper common names, often we cannot connect these
names with any known seed source. This is because many cultivars
appear for a few years in a couple of seed catalogs and then drop into
obscurity. On the other hand, users of this guide should note that in
some cases, varieties shown have no common names. The main reasons for this are the many language barriers and names that are sim-
ply too general to be useful, such as *chile verde*, which could describe
nearly every variety in existence. In South America, the common name
for all chiles is *ají*, but that term is also too general. Most cultivars
are named by their discoverer or their breeder, so we encourage gardeners to find the seed of varieties they like, grow them, and give them
a cultivar name. A friend of ours, Richard Sterling, did just that by

collecting seed for us in Cambodia and naming the cultivars 'Cambodian Flame Tongue' and 'Angkor Sunrise.' In the United States and Mexico, most varieties have specific common names, which we list.

It was not an easy task to assemble these photos. Like pepper growers everywhere, we had to combat poor germination, freezing weather, high winds, insect infestations, and diseases. In many cases we grew multiple plants of the same variety as insurance against loss, but even that effort was sometimes insufficient. We occasionally had no pods to photograph and were forced to ask our pepper-loving friends for certain photos.

We were quite fortunate to be able to collect information and seed on various trips to places around the world, including Mexico, Hungary, Thailand, Malaysia, Taiwan, Guatemala, Trinidad, Jamaica, Cayman Islands, and numerous locations in the United States. Most of the peppers in this book were grown in two areas. One was Paul Bosland's test plots and USDA seed increase plots at New Mexico State University in Las Cruces, and the other was the home garden of Dave DeWitt in the South Valley of Albuquerque. Greenhouse facilities were used at both locations, and we grew plants in both garden plots and pots. We consider this book to be the companion volume to our growing guide, *The Pepper Garden,* and so detailed gardening instructions are not provided here.

We should inform pepper lovers that genetic erosion—commonly known as extinction—of *Capsicum* varieties is taking place at an alarming rate. Habitat destruction is the leading cause of this genetic erosion, and the disappearance of *Capsicum* is directly linked to the disappearance of the rainforests where *Capsicum* originated. The genetic diversity of *Capsicum* can be saved only through the use of several strategies. One approach is to locate areas that may still harbor *Capsicum* species and protect the areas from further development. The preservation of *Capsicum* genetic resources in natural sites of occurrence must be encouraged. Whenever possible, it is desirable to set up *Capsicum* genetic resource reserves in conjunction with relevant biosphere resources and other protected areas. This is underway in Arizona, where a preserve has been established for the wild chiltepíns (see Afterword).

Another approach to preserving the genetic resources of *Capsicum* is to enlarge and conserve germ plasm in base and active gene banks. The USDA Plant Introduction Station in Georgia is a good example. It is especially important to aid the active collections of Latin America, where *Capsicum* is native.

We welcome comments from pepper growers. You can reach us at P.O. Box 4980, Albuquerque, NM 87196.

▲ ▲ ▲ ▲ ▲ ▲ ▲

Canario (Manzano) chiles in Mexico City market

▼ ▼ ▼ ▼ ▼ ▼ ▼

Peppers of the World: Identification and Breeding

Defining and identifying the Capsicums

Peppers are perennial subshrubs, native to South America, that are grown as annuals in colder climates. They are a part of the large nightshade family, or Solanaceae, and are closely related to tomatoes, potatoes, tobacco, and eggplants. They are not related to black pepper, *Piper nigrum*.

The genus *Capsicum* includes all the peppers, from the mildest bell to the hottest habanero. There are twenty-three species of *Capsicum* identified at this time, but experts continually argue about that number. The taxonomy of *Capsicum* is

Kingdom: Plantae

Division: Magnoliophyta

Class: Magnoliopsida

Order: Solanales

Family: Solanaceae

Genus: Capsicum

Species: annuum (or other species)

Pod type: Bell

Cultivar: Oriole

The pepper genus is *Capsicum*, from the Greek *kapto*, appropriately enough, meaning "to bite." The domesticated species are

annuum, meaning annual, which is an incorrect designation, as peppers are perennials. It includes most of the common varieties such as New Mexican, jalapeño, bell, and wax.

baccatum, meaning berrylike. It consists of the South American peppers commonly known as *ajís*.

chinense, meaning from China, is also an incorrect designation because the species originated in the Amazon Basin. It includes the extremely hot habaneros.

frutescens, meaning shrubby or brushy. It includes the familiar tabascos.

pubescens, meaning hairy. It includes the South American *rocotos* and the Mexican *manzanos*.

A simple key to identifying the five domesticated species of *Capsicum* follows:

DESCRIPTION	SPECIES (OR GO TO)
1. Seeds black, corolla purple	*C. pubescens*
1. Seeds tan	2
2. Corolla with spots	*C. baccatum*
2. Corolla without spots	3
3. Corolla white	4
3. Corolla greenish	5
4. Flowers solitary and filament nonpurple	*C. annuum*
4. Flowers two or more per node and filament purple	*C. chinense*
5. Flowers solitary	*C. frutescens*
5. Flowers two or more per node	*C. chinense*

How to use this guide

We have tried to be as accurate as possible in identifying the varieties, but some errors will inevitably creep into a project this large. Usually, a mistake in nomenclature is the result of mislabeled seed or an inadvertent hybrid. Nurseries and commercial greenhouses are notorious for having mislabeled or mysterious hybrids that produce unreliable results, such as two or more pod shapes on the same plant.

Each listing in this guide follows the following format:

USDA #
Botanical name:
Common name:
Location:
Seed source:
Pod length:
Pod width:
Immature color:
Mature color:
Comments:

Sometimes, information was not available to us, such as USDA number, common name, or location. The USDA number is the actual number in that agency's germ plasm bank. It can be used to request small amounts of seed (see Seed Sources). The botanical name includes genus, species, and variety (if known). The abbreviation "var." indicates a wild variety and the abbreviation "cv." means cultivated variety.

Because all *Capsicums* are Western Hemisphere crops, varieties listed from the Eastern Hemisphere have their origin in the West. We have slightly modified our original organization in *The Pepper Garden* to account for the large number of *annuum* pod types worldwide that do not fit neatly into the Western Hemisphere pod types. In this guide, the varieties are organized by similar types, roughly moving from smallest to largest pods. Our reasoning holds that the Eastern

Hemisphere peppers are so diverse that they do not fit well into the more structured pod type/variety system that works for the North and South American *annuums*. As with dogs that don't match any specific breed, peppers often do not fit neatly into a pod type designation.

As mentioned in the introduction, not all varieties have common names, but we have listed the common names that we are aware of. Regarding location, that term means where the seed we used is currently being grown. We had to be careful about listing certain locations, due to the spread of commercial seed. For example, we were excited when a friend gave us seeds from a Trinidadian farmer, and they turned out to be a classic Yucatán habanero instead of the usual red Congo pepper. When the friend checked back with the farmer, she learned that he had obtained the seeds from PetoSeed, a supplier of commercial seed. In many cases, location means origin, such as listing Yucatán as the location for classic orange habaneros. But the 'Red Savina,' although its origin is probably Caribbean, was developed in California—so that state is listed as location.

We have listed our suggested seed sources for the varieties when possible. In some cases, seed was collected on location and there is no commercial source. The two best places to check for obscure seed are the USDA and Seed Savers Exchange—both are listed under Seed Sources, page 203. Remember that commercial seed sources vary from year to year as to what they carry.

The lengths and widths of the pods can vary, but we measured what seemed to be the most typical pod on the plant. Likewise, pendancy can vary even among pods on the same plant, with some borne erect, some parallel to the ground, and some pendant. The pod colors may vary a bit, but what is described is the most typical for the variety.

The USDA "grow out"

We are fortunate to have access to a great pepper resource, the Department of Agronomy and Horticulture at New Mexico State University, where Paul is a professor. It is there that the majority of varieties in this book were grown and photographed, and we thank everyone involved in the project.

To develop new varieties, chile pepper breeders need access to diverse germ plasm with adequate documentation on their botanical and horticultural characteristics. Also, adequate seed must be made available for seed requests from growers all over the world. To accomplish these goals, the New Mexico State University Chile Breeding & Genetics Program has cooperated with the USDA Southern Plant Introduction Station for more than seven years in increasing and evaluating *Capsicum* germ plasm.

Each year, between 250 and 500 accessions of *Capsicum* are chosen from the USDA collection for seed increase. Detailed evaluation information is collected, and each accession is monitored for correct plant species designation. The NMSU program collects forty-one descriptors for each accession, including fruit shape, fruit size, immature and mature fruit color, pungency, and many more.

To increase the USDA *Capsicum* collection, the NMSU program uses cloth isolation cages with a minimum of sixty plants to provide adequate genetic stability of the varieties. The fruit is hand-harvested when ripe, and the seed extracted, cleaned, packaged, and provided to the USDA Southern Plant Introduction Station for storage and distribution. The data collected is then sent to the USDA Southern Plant Introduction Station for transmittal to the Germplasm Resources Information Network (GRIN).

GRIN is a centralized computer database system that manages plant genetic resources. It is through GRIN that scientists can locate plants with specific characteristics and then obtain them for research purposes. The database is designed to permit flexibility to users in retrieving information.

The login identification and an access code or pcGRIN diskettes may be obtained by any plant scientist, plant breeder, or research organization. Requests should be sent to: The Database Manager, GRIN DataBase Management Unit (DBMU), USDA/ARS/PSI/NGRL, Building 003, Room 003, BARC-West, Beltsville, MD 20705-2350.

A WEB site is available at www.ars-grin.gov. This address goes to the home page of the National Plant Germplasm System. Once there, choose the "plants" option. There it is possible to FTP or download the pcGRIN manual or the pcGRIN for *Capsicum*.

Saving seed

One of the most commonly asked questions about *Capsicum* cultivation is, Can I save seed? The answer is yes, but of course there are qualifications to that statement. First, chile plants will cross-pollinate, meaning that bees or insects visiting the flowers will bring pollen from other varieties. This will cause outcrossing. Outcrossing is common enough that isolation by distance or netting is required for pure seed production. However, if you have only one plant or several plants of only one variety, then saving seed will work as long as your neighbor is not growing peppers as well. If the plants you grow are not hybrids, it is much more likely that the offspring will look like the parents. However, if you are saving seed from plants that are hybrid plants, the seed will not necessarily produce plants with fruits like those from which you saved the seeds. If you are willing to experiment, you can plant the seeds from the hybrids and see the various fruit shapes and colors they produce.

Thus, one must know whether the variety is a hybrid or an open-pollinated (OP) cultivar. If an OP cultivar is kept isolated from different

Chile ristras

plants with which they can cross, they will produce seed that will come true to type. However, if the cultivar is an F_1 hybrid, saving seed is chancy. An F_1 hybrid is the seed from two genetically different parents. The parents can be very different or very similar, and technically, the two parents only have to differ by one gene to be labeled an F_1 hybrid.

Hybrids can be superior to OP cultivars. They are often more uniform and sometimes have greater vigor and yield. But commercial hybrids are developed for another reason. A seed company puts a lot of resources into developing a new cultivar, and they want to protect their investment. If a gardener or farmer saves his own seed, the seed company will not profit. Thus, the seed companies use F_1 hybrids to keep individuals from saving seed.

However, "dehybridizing" the F_1 hybrids is a legal and interesting endeavor. Professional plant breeders have bred a number of beneficial qualities into the hybrids, such as disease and pest resistance and new fruit colors. So one can select individuals and turn them into an OP cultivar. The uniformity of hybrids is sometimes not desirable for home gardeners. To have fruits produced over a longer period of time, instead of one big flush of fruits, can be an advantage. After your new OP cultivar is developed, remember that you must keep it isolated from other pepper plants to produce genetically pure seed.

Creating pepper hybrids

Pollination, or sexual reproduction, is the uniting of male and female gametes or reproductive cells. From this union, a seed is produced. Flowers begin to form when the pepper plant branches. Flowering is dichotomous, meaning that one flower forms, then two, then four, then eight, and so on. The number of flowers produced is very large compared to those that actually set fruit, and a larger percentage of the early flowers set fruit than the later flowers. The key factor affecting fruit set is night temperature, which ideally should be between 65° and 80°F. Fruit will not set when the temperature is above 85° at night because of excessive transpiration, which causes the blossoms to drop. Blossoms also drop because of excessive nitrogen, high winds, or lack of pollination. If daytime temperatures exceed 95°,

Orange veins of chile, where pungency is located

pollen will abort and the fruit set will be reduced. In some cases, spraying hormones—such as Bloom Set®—on the flowers may prevent blossom drop.

Flowers of peppers are perfect, meaning that each flower has both male and female organs. The sexual organs are easy to distinguish, so crossing peppers is relatively easy. Pollination is the transfer of pollen from an anther to a stigma. When the anther is mature, it opens and releases pollen. Pollen may be transferred in two ways: cross-pollination and self-pollination.

In cross-pollination, the pollen is transferred from an anther of one plant to a stigma of another plant. In self-pollination, the pollen is transferred from an anther to the stigma of the same flower, or to the stigma of another flower on the same plant.

Early botanists grew peppers in greenhouses. Without insects, the peppers self-pollinated. Thus in earlier literature, peppers were considered to be self-pollinating. Peppers do self-pollinate, but their ability to cross-pollinate is far greater than expected. Cross-pollination is quite common in peppers grown outdoors. Studies have indicated that 30 to 70 percent of pepper flowers will cross-pollinate, depending on location and season. There is a much higher percentage of natural cross-pollination in peppers than in tomatoes.

Cross-pollination in peppers is enhanced by the structure of the pepper flower because the extended styles and the presence of nectar encourage insects to visit the flower and aid in cross-pollination. Because of genetic recombination, plants originating from seed can be quite different from the parent and from each other. Plant breeders can therefore develop new cultivars with sexual reproduction. It is important to remember that if pure seed is to be saved, the flowers should *not* be allowed to cross-pollinate.

Making your own pepper crosses

Pepper breeders make controlled crosses between plants in order to combine genes of interest, and with a little practice you too can make your own crosses.

Step 1. Select the flower bud.

Select a flower bud that has not opened. A pepper flower has both male (stamens, consisting of anther and filament) and female (pistil) reproductive organs. Selecting an unopened flower bud reduces the chance for self-pollination.

Step 2. Open the flower bud.

Using forceps or tweezers, carefully remove the petals from the flower bud to expose the reproductive organs.

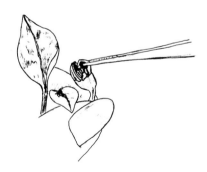

Step 3. Emasculate the flower.

The male parts of the flower are composed of anthers attached to small filaments. Pollen is produced in the anther. In order to prevent self-pollination, the anthers must be removed. Remove them, but be sure to leave the central pistil in place.

Step 4. Collect pollen.

Collect pollen from the open flower of another pepper plant. A small paintbrush or a bee stick can be used to collect and transfer the pollen.

Step 5. Pollinate the flower.

Transfer the pollen to the tip (stigma) of the pistil.

Step 6. Label the cross.

Label the cross so that it may be identified as the fruit matures. The fruit will look like all the other fruit on the plant because the cross resides in the growing seeds, not in this year's pod shape.

After the fruit ripens, harvest the seed and plant it as you would any seed. Remember to label the cross in the garden. You will be able to see the results of your cross as the seeds grow into mature plants.

The Wild Species:
Undomesticated *Capsicums*

W E TEND TO THINK OF PEPPERS as annual, domesticated crops, but in reality all chiles are perennials and numerous varieties grow wild, needing no help from humans to proliferate. On our travels throughout the world we have found wild chiles growing in many different locales. They all have one thing in common: an association with birds.

Bird peppers

According to botanists, the genus *Capsicum*, to which all chiles belong, originated in the remote geologic past in an area bordered by the mountains of southern Brazil to the east, by Bolivia to the west, and by Paraguay and northern Argentina to the south. Not only does this location have the greatest concentration of wild species of chiles in the world, but here, and only here, grow representatives of all the major domesticated species within the genus. Some botanists believe that the location for the origin of chile peppers was further east, in central Bolivia along the Rio Grande.

Scientists are not certain about the exact time frame or the method for the spread of both wild and domesticated species from the southern Brazil-Bolivia area, but they suspect that birds were primarily responsible. The wild chiles (as well as their undomesticated cousin of today, the chiltepín) had erect, red fruits that were quite pungent and were very attractive to various species of birds that ate the whole pods. The seeds of those pods passed through their digestive tracts intact and were deposited on the ground encased in a perfect fertilizer.

Flower of *C. praetermissum*, USDA #441654

In this manner, chiles spread all over South and Central America long before the first Asian peoples crossed the Bering land bridge and settled the Western Hemisphere. The small pods of the undomesticated species are commonly called "bird peppers" in languages all over the world, and we describe the wild varieties of the domesticated species in the appropriate chapters.

Botanists believe that birds are immune from the capsaicin (pungency) in the pods and that the chemical evolved to protect chile peppers from mammalian predators. Scientists have long speculated that plants produce secondary metabolites, chemicals that are not required for the primary life support of the plant, to fight off predators and perhaps even competing plant species.

Capsaicin in chiles may be such a metabolite. It prevents animals from eating the chiles, so that they can be consumed by fruit-eating birds who specialize in red fruits with small seeds. Mammals perceive a burning sensation from capsaicin, but birds do not.

Development of the Capsicum species

When humans arrived in the Americas more than ten thousand years ago, about twenty-five species of the genus *Capsicum* existed in South America. Five of these species were later domesticated; however, some of the other wild species were and still are occasionally utilized by humans. The first humans in the Western Hemisphere probably used chiles as a medicinal plant, a use still practiced today. The early civilizations in the Western Hemisphere did not recognize separate species within *Capsicum*. Nonetheless, they did recognize different pod types and selected for specific cuisine uses. After Columbus and the spread of chiles through Europe, Africa, and Asia, botantists began to classify the chile types into species. At first, each pod type was considered a species. As the concept of biological species became more accepted, the *Capsicum* genus was reduced to the ones known today.

Two of the five domesticated species of chiles, C. *baccatum* and C. *pubescens*, never migrated beyond South America. C. *baccatum*, known as *ají*, extended its range from southern Brazil west to the Pacific Ocean, and became a domesticated chile of choice in Bolivia, Ecuador, Peru, and Chile. Likewise, C. *pubescens* left Brazil to be domesticated in the Andes, where it is known as *rocoto*. Its range today is primarily in the higher elevations of Bolivia, Peru, and Ecuador, although it was introduced during historical times into mountainous areas of Costa Rica, Honduras, Guatemala, and Mexico.

Three other *Capsicum* species that were later domesticated are *annuum, chinense,* and *frutescens.* These closely related species shared a mutual, ancestral gene pool and are known to botanists as the *annuum-chinense-frutescens* complex. They seem to have sprung up in the wilds of Colombia and later migrated individually to Central America and Amazonia. These three species were all in place when humans arrived on the scene, and, apparently, each type was domesticated independently—*annuum* in Mexico, *chinense* in Amazonia (or possibly Peru), and *frutescens* in southern Central America. These three species have become the most commercially important peppers.

Not every wild *Capsicum* species is shown in this chapter because some of the species may very well be extinct. Nevertheless, the wild species share similiar fruit traits. The fruits are small, with a soft pedicel trait that allows the red ripe fruit to be pulled easily from the calyx. This permits frugivorous birds to eat the fruit with ease, and disseminate the seeds.

▼ ▼ ▼ ▼ ▼ ▼ ▼ ▼ ▼ ▼ ▼

USDA # 573336

Botanical name: *Capsicum cardenasii*

Common name: ulupica

Location: Bolivia

Seed source: USDA

Pod length: .25 in.

Pod width: .25 in.

Immature color: green

Mature color: red

Comments: Flower blue with cream-colored spots. Very pungent.

▼ ▼ ▼ ▼ ▼ ▼ ▼ ▼ ▼ ▼ ▼

USDA #439414

Botanical name: *Capsicum chacoense*

Common name: unknown

Location: Argentina

Seed source: USDA

Pod length: .25 in.

Pod width: .125 in.

Immature color: green

Mature color: red

Comments: White flower; pods very deciduous. This photo shows how pods cluster. Very pungent.

▼ ▼ ▼ ▼ ▼ ▼ ▼ ▼ ▼ ▼

USDA #439415

Botanical name: *Capsicum chacoense*

Common name: unknown

Location: Bolivia

Seed source: USDA

Pod length: .25 in.

Pod width: .125 in.

Immature color: green

Mature color: red

Comments: White flower. This photo shows individual pod detail. Very pungent.

▼ ▼ ▼ ▼ ▼ ▼ ▼ ▼ ▼ ▼

USDA #GRIF 1567

Botanical name: *Capsicum galapagoense*

Common name: unknown

Location: Galapagos Islands

Seed source: USDA

Pod length: .25 in.

Pod width: .12 in.

Immature color: dark green

Mature color: red

Comments: Endemic on the Galapagos Islands. Very pungent.

▼ ▼ ▼ ▼ ▼ ▼ ▼ ▼ ▼ ▼

USDA #441654

Botanical name: *Capsicum praetermissum*

Common name: unknown

Location: Brazil

Seed source: USDA

Pod length: .25 in.

Pod width: .25 in.

Immature color: green

Mature color: red

Comments: Flower purple with yellow spots. Very pungent.

Tabascos and More:
Capsicum frutescens

THE TABASCO PEPPER IS THE BEST-KNOWN cultivar of this species, being the primary ingredient in the famous sauce that is now more than 125 years old. Another famous variety is the *malagueta*, which grows wild in the Amazon Basin in Brazil, where the species probably originated. Curiously, there are not as many names for the undomesticated varieties of *frutescens* as there are for the undomesticated varieties of other species. The most common name is bird pepper. No domesticated *C. frutescens* has ever been found in an archaeological site in Central or South America, but ethnobotanists speculate the domestication site was probably Panama, and from there it spread to Mexico and the Caribbean.

At any rate, we know the tabasco variety of *C. frutescens* was being cultivated near Tabasco, Mexico, in the early 1840s because it was transferred to Louisiana in 1848, where it was eventually grown to produce Tabasco sauce. Demand outstripped supply, and today tabascos are commercially grown in Central America and Colombia and shipped in mash form to Louisiana.

In Louisiana, tabasco peppers fell victim to the tobacco etch virus, but were rescued in 1970 with the introduction of 'Greenleaf Tabasco,' a TEV-resistant variety. Today at Avery Island, the site of the original tabasco growing and manufacturing operation, there are still fields of tabasco under cultivation—but mostly for crop improvement and seed production.

An interesting botanical mystery surfaces with the malagueta pepper from Brazil because it has virtually the same name as the

LEFT: The wild—and occasionally cultivated—malagueta

MIDDLE: *C. frutescens* flower. This photograph shows the erect pedicel and green color.

BOTTOM: A maturing Tabasco plant

melegueta pepper from West Africa. The mystery arises from the fact that the two peppers are completely unrelated botanically and in appearance. The African melegueta (*Aframomum melegueta*) is a reed-like plant with red berries, while the Brazilian malagueta is very similar to the tabasco chile.

The melegueta pepper enjoyed great popularity during the Elizabethan Age in England, primarily through trade with Portugal. Some food historians believe that because the word melegueta was already a Portuguese term for spicy berry, this name was transferred to a Brazilian red chile pepper of even more pungency sometime after the Portuguese settlement of Brazil. This scenario follows a pattern that Christopher Columbus began when he misnamed chiles as peppers. The chile peppers, it seems, were given the closest common name when the Europeans were introduced to them. Interestingly enough, the African meleguetas were eventually imported into Surinam and Guyana, where they were grown commercially.

Some varieties of *C. frutescens* found their way to India and the Far East, where they are still called bird pepper. There they are cultivated to make hot sauces and curries.

C. frutescens plants have a compact habit, an intermediate number of stems, and grow between 1 and 4 feet high, depending on climate and growing conditions. Their leaves are ovate, smooth, and measure 2.5 inches long and 2 inches wide.

The flowers have greenish white corollas with no spots, and purple anthers. The pods are borne erect and measure up to 1.5 inches long and .25 inches wide. Immature pods are yellow or green, maturing to bright red. The *frutescens* species is quite hot, measuring between 30,000 and 50,000 Scoville heat units.

The height of the plants depends on climate, with the plants growing the largest in warmer parts of the country. They are particularly good for container gardening, and one of our specimens lived as a perennial for four years in a pot, but gradually lost vigor and produced fewer pods each year. A single plant can produce a hundred or more pods.

The species *C. frutescens* and *C. pubescens* have fewer pod shapes, sizes, and colors than *C. annuum, C. chinense,* and *C. baccatum.*

No one knows the real reason for this. One must remember that the diversity of pod shapes is human guided. In other words, the differences one sees in pod size and shape are because humans conscientiously made choices about which pods to save for the next growing season. In nature, wild chile plants usually have small, red, erect fruits that drop off easily. The small fruit and easy fruit drop traits are beneficial for bird dispersal. However, humans prefer large fruit and fruit that stays attached to the plant until harvested. Thus, under domestication these traits are modified.

The *C. frutescens* plant has small fruits that drop off easily. Therefore, an explanation for the lack of fruit shapes in *C. frutescens* is that it is still mostly a wild form. It is found growing in the same areas as *C. annuum* and *C. chinense*, so selection may have been on *C. annuum* and *C. chinense*, while *C. frutescens* had little or no selection.

The most common use for the pods is making hot sauces; they are crushed, salted, fermented, and combined with vinegar. However, the pods can be used fresh in salsas and can be dried for adding to stir-fry dishes.

▼ ▼ ▼ ▼ ▼ ▼ ▼ ▼ ▼ ▼

USDA # none

Botanical name: *Capsicum frutescens*

Common name: wild tabasco

Location: Costa Rica

Seed source: collected in the wild

Pod length: .75 in.

Pod width: .25 in.

Immature color: yellow

Mature color: red

Comments: Our knowledgeable guides in Costa Rica called this "wild tabasco."

▼ ▼ ▼ ▼ ▼ ▼ ▼ ▼ ▼ ▼

USDA # none

Botanical name: *Capsicum frutescens* cv. 'Diente de Perro'

Common name: dog's tooth

Location: Guatemala

Seed source: Seed Savers Exchange

Pod length: 1 in.

Pod width: .25 in.

Immature color: green

Mature color: red

Comments: A frutescens cultivated in home gardens.

▼ ▼ ▼ ▼ ▼ ▼ ▼ ▼ ▼ ▼

USDA #497984

Botanical name: *Capsicum frutescens* var. *malagueta*

Common name: malagueta pepper

Location: Brazil

Seed source: USDA

Pod length: .75 in.

Pod width: .25 in.

Immature color: green

Mature color: red

Comments: This variety grows wild in the Amazon basin, but also is cultivated in small home plots. It has a green corolla.

▼ ▼ ▼ ▼ ▼ ▼ ▼ ▼ ▼ ▼ ▼

USDA #439493

Botanical name: *Capsicum frutescens*

Common name: unknown

Location: Colombia

Seed source: USDA

Pod length: 1 in.

Pod width: .25 in.

Immature color: green

Mature color: red-orange

Comments: Characteristic green flower. Has some *C. chinense* traits.

▼ ▼ ▼ ▼ ▼ ▼ ▼ ▼ ▼ ▼ ▼

USDA #441687

Botanical name: *Capsicum frutescens*

Common name: unknown

Location: Brazil

Seed source: USDA

Pod length: .5 in.

Pod width: .25 in.

Immature color: green

Mature color: red

Comments: A vigorous grower.

▼ ▼ ▼ ▼ ▼ ▼ ▼ ▼ ▼ ▼

USDA #260480

Botanical name: *Capsicum frutescens* cv. 'Ají Chuncho'

Common name: ají chuncho

Location: Peru

Seed source: USDA

Pod length: .75 in.

Pod width: .5 in.

Immature color: green

Mature color: red

Comments: Could be a wild *C. chinense.*

▼ ▼ ▼ ▼ ▼ ▼ ▼ ▼ ▼ ▼

USDA # none

Botanical name: *Capsicum frutescens* cv. 'Zimbabwe Bird'

Common name: Zimbabwe bird pepper

Location: Zimbabwe

Seed source: Redwood City Seed Co.

Pod length: 1.25 in.

Pod width: .5 in.

Immature color: light green

Mature color: red

Comments: Flower color is green.

▼ ▼ ▼ ▼ ▼ ▼ ▼ ▼ ▼ ▼ ▼

USDA # none

Botanical name: *Capsicum frutescens* cv. 'Wild Grove'

Common name: wild grove

Location: not known

Seed source: The Pepper Gal

Pod length: 1 in.

Pod width: .25 in.

Immature color: yellow-green

Mature color: red

Comments: Ornamental, similar to tabasco.

▼ ▼ ▼ ▼ ▼ ▼ ▼ ▼ ▼ ▼ ▼

USDA # none

Botanical name: *Capsicum frutescens* cv. 'Angkor Sunrise'

Common name: Angkor sunrise

Location: Cambodia

Seed source: collected in Cambodia

Pod length: 1 in.

Pod width: .5 in.

Immature color: yellow

Mature color: red

Comments: Seed collected in Cambodia by Richard Sterling.

▼ ▼ ▼ ▼ ▼ ▼ ▼ ▼ ▼ ▼ ▼

USDA # none

Botanical name: *Capsicum frutescens* cv. 'Tabasco'

Common name: tabasco

Location: Louisiana and Mexico

Seed source: Enchanted Seeds

Pod length: 2.5–3 in.

Pod width: .8 in.

Immature color: green

Mature color: red

Comments: Flower color green; used to make the famous hot sauce

▼ ▼ ▼ ▼ ▼ ▼ ▼ ▼ ▼ ▼ ▼

USDA # none

Botanical name: *Capsicum frutescens* cv. 'Greenleaf Tabasco'

Common name: tabasco

Location: Auburn University, Alabama

Seed source: Enchanted Seeds

Pod length: 1.25 in.

Pod width: .5 in.

Immature color: yellow

Mature color: red

Comments: Bred for resistance to tobacco etch virus.

▲▲▲▲▲▲▲

Market scene with chiles, Guatemala

▼▼▼▼▼▼▼

Rocotos and Canarios:
Capsicum pubescens

C. PUBESCENS IS THE ONLY DOMESTICATED species with no wild form; however, two wild species, *C. cardenasii* and *C. eximium*, are closely related. The center of origin for this species was Bolivia, and it was probably domesticated about 6,000 B.C., making it one of the oldest domesticated plants in the Americas. Botanist Charles Heiser, citing Garcilaso de la Vega (1609), notes that *C. pubescens* was "the most common pepper among the Incas, just as it is today in Cuzco, the former capital of the Incan empire."

It is grown today in the Andes from Chile to Colombia, mostly in small family plots. It is also cultivated in highland areas of Central America and Mexico. The common name for this species in South America is *rocoto* or *locoto*. In Mexico, it is also called *chile manzano* (apple pepper), and *chile perón* (pear pepper), allusions to its fruitlike shapes. In some parts of Mexico and Guatemala, *pubescens* is called *chile caballo* (horse pepper). Yellow *C. pubescens* is called *canarios*, or canaries, in parts of Mexico, particularly Oaxaca, and some parts of Central America.

C. pubescens has a compact to erect habit (sometimes sprawling and vinelike) and grows up to 4 feet tall, but 2 feet is more usual in U.S. gardens. In Bolivia and Guatemala, they grow to 15 feet. The leaves are ovate, light to dark green, very pubescent (hairy), and measure up to 3.5 inches long and 2 inches wide.

The flowers have purple corollas, purple and white anthers, and stand erect above the leaves. The pods are round, sometimes pear shaped, measuring about 2 to 3 inches long and 2 to 2.5 inches wide,

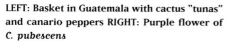

LEFT: Basket in Guatemala with cactus "tunas" and canario peppers RIGHT: Purple flower of *C. pubescens*

but some pods as large as bell peppers have been reported. The pods are green in their immature state, maturing to yellow, orange, or red.

Their heat level is 30,000 to 50,000 Scoville heat units and higher. The *C. pubescens* varieties contain a unique set of capsaicinoids (pungency compounds), causing some people to believe they are hotter than habaneros. In parts of the Americas they are referred to as *el mas picante de los picantes* (the hottest of the hot). But they are not as pungent as the hottest *C. chinense*.

As with *C. frutescens*, there is a lack of pod diversity within *C. pubescens*. The fruits are large and stay attached to the plant. No wild plant with small fruits that easily separate from the plant has ever been found. It has been suggested that *C. pubescens* was domesticated so long ago that its wild form is extinct. But, then, why is the variability less? One explanation is that when *C. pubescens* was domesticated it went through a founder's effect, a situation that occurs when the establishment of a new population is founded by a few original individuals that carry only a small fraction of the total genetic variation of the parental population. If this was the case, there is not enough genetic diversity to allow for genetic recombination to produce the assortment of pod forms seen in the other species.

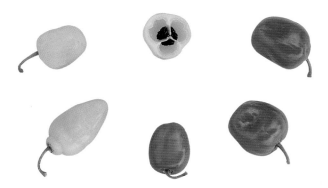

Black seeds are characteristic of this species.

Furthermore, *C. pubescens* is isolated from other domesticated species and cannot cross-pollinate with them. This reduces the genes available. Another factor may be the climate it grows best in. Because it thrives only in a narrow temperature range, it may not have been grown in as many places, thus reducing the opportunity for selection by humans.

Scientists are presently addressing this question with sophisticated molecular techniques. Their work may make it possible for us to have an answer in a few years to the question of lack of pod diversity. Of course, their work depends on having the genetic resources available—the seeds of the future.

The *C. pubescens* are traditionally grown in high mountainous areas of tropical countries. They can survive very light frosts but not hard freezes. Some sources state that because of their long growing season and need for long days, the *C. pubescens* varieties are unsuitable for cultivation in the United States. However, our experiments have shown that plants started early can achieve fruiting in one season. Some plants may not fruit because there is self-incompatibility in the species. To set fruit, pollen must be transferred by bees or humans from a neighboring plant of the same variety. The species also responds well to shading because the foliage has a tendency to burn in full sun. The growing season is long, 120 days or more, and the plants produce up to thirty pods, depending on the length of the growing season.

Leaves illustrating pubescent trait

Because it is adapted to the cooler highland temperatures, C. *pubescens* grows best under cooler conditions. This can be a cool coastal climate, a mountain garden, or an artificial climate, such as a greenhouse. In southern New Mexico, the summer heat is too strong to get good growth on the plants, as the leaves tend to burn. All C. *pubescens* plants are grown in a greenhouse that has evaporative coolers to keep the temperature within an adequate range. The seeds are sterilized with sodium hypochlorite, then planted in plastic trays. After planting, the trays are watered as needed to maintain optimum plant growth, usually a once-a-day watering. The trays are placed on a greenhouse bench where the air temperature is maintained at 80°F during the day, and 55° at night. The seedlings are thinned to the most vigorous plant per cell.

Once the seedlings have six to eight true leaves, they are transplanted to pots. Either two plants are planted in an 8-inch pot or a single plant to a 6-inch pot. Fertilizer is kept to a minimum because C. *pubescens* plants, if given too much nitrogen, will grow profusely without flowering and consequently without setting fruit. Plants can live for several years in a pot.

C. *pubescens* varieties are usually consumed in their fresh form because the pods are so thick they are difficult to dry. They are commonly used in fresh salsas, and the larger pods can be stuffed with meat or cheese and baked.

▼ ▼ ▼ ▼ ▼ ▼ ▼ ▼ ▼ ▼ ▼

USDA # none

Botanical name: *Capsicum pubescens* cv. 'Canario'

Common names: rocoto, caballo, canario

Location: Costa Rica, Mexico, and Guatemala

Seed source: Enchanted Seeds

Pod length: 1.75 in.

Pod width: 1.25 in.

Immature color: green

Mature color: yellow, occasionally red

Comments: Canario is common name for the yellow form.

▼ ▼ ▼ ▼ ▼ ▼ ▼ ▼ ▼ ▼ ▼

USDA # none

Botanical name: *Capsicum pubescens* cv. 'Rocoto'

Common names: rocoto, manzano

Location: Peru

Seed source: Enchanted Seeds

Pod length: 1.75 in.

Pod width: 1.25 in.

Immature color: green

Mature color: red

Comments: Sometimes these pods are quite large. High pungency. Note the apple-like shape.

▲ ▲ ▲ ▲ ▲ ▲ ▲

Unloading cayenne peppers, St. Martinville, Louisiana

▼ ▼ ▼ ▼ ▼ ▼ ▼

Los Ajís of South America:
Capsicum baccatum

T HE *C. BACCATUM* SPECIES, familiarly termed ají throughout South
America, originated in either Bolivia or Peru and, according to
archaeological evidence, was probably domesticated in Peru about
2,500 B.C. Extensive *C. baccatum* material found at the Huaca Prieta
archaeological site in Peru shows that the species was gradually
improved by the pre-Incan civilizations. Fruit size increased and the
fruits gradually became nondeciduous and stayed on the plants
through ripening. There are at least two wild forms (varieties *baccatum* and *microcarpum*) and many domesticated forms. The domesticated ajís have a great diversity of pod shape and size, ranging from
short, pointed pods borne erect to long, pendant pods resembling the
New Mexican cultivars. One variety of ají, *puca-uchu,* grows on a
vinelike plant in home gardens. The *C. baccatum* species is generally
distinguished from the other species by the yellow or tan spots on the
corollas, and by the yellow anthers.

Baccatums are cultivated in Argentina, Colombia, Ecuador, Peru,
Brazil, and Bolivia, and the species has been introduced into Costa
Rica, India, and the United States. In the United States, it is grown to
a very limited extent in California under the brand name Mild Italian
and in Nevada under the brand name Chileno.

The baccatums are tall (sometimes reaching 5 feet), have multiple
stems, and an erect habit, occasionally tending toward sprawling. The
large leaves are dark green, measuring up to 7 inches long and 4 inches
wide. The *C. baccatum* plants tend to stand out in the garden like
small trees. Their growing period is up to 120 days or more, and the
plants can produce forty or more pods.

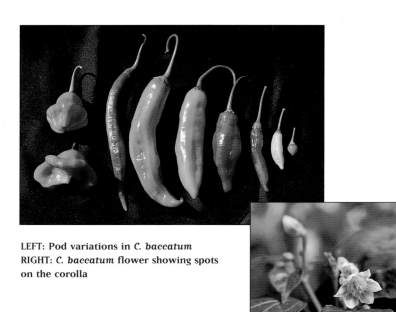

LEFT: Pod variations in *C. baccatum*
RIGHT: *C. baccatum* flower showing spots
on the corolla

The flower corollas are white with distinctive dark green or brown spots; anthers are yellow or tan. The pods usually begin erect and become pendant as they mature, are elongate in shape, and measure between 3 to 6 inches long and .75 to 1.5 inches wide. They usually mature to an orange red, but yellow and brown colors also appear in some varieties. The pods usually measure between 30,000 and 50,000 Scoville heat units.

The pods have a distinctive, fruity flavor and are used fresh in ceviche (lime-marinated fish) in South America. They are also used in fresh salsas. The pods of all ajís are dried in the sun and then crushed into colorful powders.

In *Chile Pepper* magazine, Mary Dempsey noted that "ají is called 'ají amarillo' when it is yellow or orange and 'ají colorado' when red. When dried, it is often referred to as 'cuzqueño,' after the city of Cuzco. Piles of the orange, gold, and brilliant-red peppers are found in every outdoor market in Peru, tossed in jumbled piles, or divided by color upon handwoven cloths."

▼ ▼ ▼ ▼ ▼ ▼ ▼ ▼ ▼ ▼

USDA #238061

Botanical name: *Capsicum baccatum* var. *baccatum*

Common name: bird ají

Location: Bolivia

Seed source: USDA, Seed Savers Exchange

Pod length: .5 in.

Pod width: .3 in.

Immature color: green

Mature color: red

Comments: Wild variety, very hot, very prolific. Spreading habit.

▼ ▼ ▼ ▼ ▼ ▼ ▼ ▼ ▼ ▼

USDA #439361

Botanical name: *Capsicum baccatum*

Common name: unknown

Location: Bolivia

Seed source: USDA

Pod length: .5 in.

Pod width: .25 in.

Immature color: green

Mature color: red

Comments: Possibly a wild variety.

▼ ▼ ▼ ▼ ▼ ▼ ▼ ▼ ▼ ▼

USDA #159252

Botanical name: *Capsicum baccatum*

Common name: unknown

Location: United States

Seed source: USDA

Pod length: .5 in.

Pod width: .5 in.

Immature color: yellow

Mature color: red

Comments: Flower white with green spots.

▼ ▼ ▼ ▼ ▼ ▼ ▼ ▼ ▼ ▼

USDA #260434

Botanical name: *Capsicum baccatum*

Common name: unknown

Location: Bolivia

Seed source: USDA

Pod length: .75 in.

Pod width: .25 in.

Immature color: yellow

Mature color: orange

Comments: Flower white with yellow spots.

▼ ▼ ▼ ▼ ▼ ▼ ▼ ▼ ▼ ▼

USDA #439361

Botanical name: *Capsicum baccatum*

Common name: unknown

Location: Mexico

Seed source: USDA

Pod length: 1.5 in.

Pod width: .5 in.

Immature color: green

Mature color: red

Comments: Flower white with yellow spots.

▼ ▼ ▼ ▼ ▼ ▼ ▼ ▼ ▼ ▼

USDA #439384

Botanical name: *Capsicum baccatum*

Common name: unknown

Location: Peru

Seed source: USDA

Pod length: .75 in.

Pod width: .25 in.

Immature color: green

Mature color: red

Comments: Flower white with yellow spots.

▼ ▼ ▼ ▼ ▼ ▼ ▼ ▼ ▼ ▼ ▼

USDA #439380

Botanical name: *Capsicum baccatum*

Common name: unknown

Location: Mexico

Seed source: USDA

Pod length: .25 in.

Pod width: .5 in.

Immature color: green

Mature color: red

Comments: White flower with yellow spots.

▼ ▼ ▼ ▼ ▼ ▼ ▼ ▼ ▼ ▼ ▼

USDA # none

Botanical name: *Capsicum baccatum* cv. 'Valentine'

Common name: valentine ají

Location: South America

Seed source: Seed Savers Exchange

Pod length: .5 in.

Pod width: .4 in.

Immature color: green

Mature color: red

Comments: Medium heat. Prolific. Pods are both erect and pendant.

▼ ▼ ▼ ▼ ▼ ▼ ▼ ▼ ▼ ▼

USDA #370004

Botanical name: *Capsicum baccatum*

Common name: unknown

Location: India

Seed source: USDA

Pod length: 2 in.

Pod width: .5 in.

Immature color: green

Mature color: red

Comments: Flower white with yellow spots. Pods horizontal.

▼ ▼ ▼ ▼ ▼ ▼ ▼ ▼ ▼ ▼

USDA #260593

Botanical name: *Capsicum baccatum*

Common name: malagueta (could be a misnomer)

Location: Brazil

Seed source: USDA

Pod length: 1 in.

Pod width: .25 in.

Immature color: green

Mature color: red

Comments: Flower white with green spots. Malagueta usually refers to *C. frutescens*.

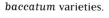

USDA #439368

Botanical name: *Capsicum baccatum*

Common name: unknown

Location: Brazil

Seed source: USDA

Pod length: .75 in.

Pod width: 1.5 in.

Immature color: green

Mature color: red

Comments: Brazil has a large number of *C. baccatum* varieties.

USDA #439370

Botanical name: *Capsicum baccatum*

Common name: unknown

Location: Bulgaria

Seed source: USDA

Pod length: 1 in.

Pod width: .75 in.

Immature color: yellow

Mature color: red

Comments: Flower white with yellow spots. Note unique pod shape. Horizontal growth.

▼ ▼ ▼ ▼ ▼ ▼ ▼ ▼ ▼ ▼ ▼

USDA # 439409

Botanical name: *Capsicum baccatum*

Common name: unknown

Location: Uruguay

Seed source: USDA

Pod length: 1.5 in.

Pod width: 1.25 in.

Immature color: green

Mature color: red

Comments: Flower white with yellow spots.

▼ ▼ ▼ ▼ ▼ ▼ ▼ ▼ ▼ ▼

USDA #439382

Botanical name: *Capsicum baccatum*

Common name: unknown

Location: Paraguay

Seed source: USDA

Pod length: .75 in.

Pod width: .5 in.

Immature color: green

Mature color: red

Comments: Flower white with yellow spots.

▼ ▼ ▼ ▼ ▼ ▼ ▼ ▼ ▼ ▼

USDA #441583

Botanical name: *Capsicum baccatum*

Common name: unknown

Location: Brazil

Seed source: USDA

Pod length: .75 in.

Pod width: .75 in.

Immature color: green

Mature color: red

Comments: Flower cream with yellow spots.

▼ ▼ ▼ ▼ ▼ ▼ ▼ ▼ ▼ ▼

USDA #497973

Botanical name: *Capsicum baccatum* cv. 'Pilange'

Common name: ají pilange

Location: Brazil

Seed source: USDA

Pod length: .75 in.

Pod width: 1.5 in.

Immature color: green

Mature color: red

Comments: White flower with yellow spots.

▼ ▼ ▼ ▼ ▼ ▼ ▼ ▼ ▼ ▼

USDA #439381

Botanical name: *Capsicum baccatum*

Common name: unknown

Location: Mexico

Seed source: USDA

Pod length: 1.25 in.

Pod width: .25 in.

Immature color: green

Mature color: red

Comments: White flower with yellow spots.

▼ ▼ ▼ ▼ ▼ ▼ ▼ ▼ ▼ ▼

USDA #446900

Botanical name: *Capsicum baccatum*

Common name: unknown

Location: Peru

Seed source: USDA

Pod length: 2 in.

Pod width: .75 in.

Immature color: green

Mature color: orange

Comments: White flower with brown spots.

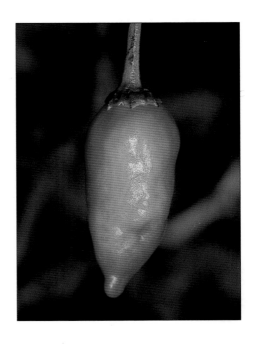

▼ ▼ ▼ ▼ ▼ ▼ ▼ ▼ ▼ ▼

USDA #439411

Botanical name: *Capsicum baccatum*

Common name: unknown

Location: Uruguay

Seed source: USDA

Pod length: 1.25 in.

Pod width: 1 in.

Immature color: green

Mature color: red

Comments: White flower with yellow spots.

▼ ▼ ▼ ▼ ▼ ▼ ▼ ▼ ▼ ▼

USDA #497974

Botanical name: *Capsicum baccatum* cv. 'Peri-Peri'

Common names: peri-peri, orchid

Location: Portugal

Seed source: Seed Savers Exchange

Pod length: 2 in.

Pod width: 2.5 in.

Immature color: green

Mature color: orange or red

Comments: Mild heat. Very flavorful. Often misidentified as a habanero. Originated in South America, transferred to Europe by the Portuguese.

▼ ▼ ▼ ▼ ▼ ▼ ▼ ▼ ▼ ▼

USDA #273420

Botanical name: *Capsicum baccatum* cv. 'Christmas Bell'

Common name: Christmas bell ají

Location: South America

Seed source: Seed Savers Exchange

Pod length: 1.75 in.

Pod width: 1.25 in.

Immature color: green

Mature color: yellow or red

Comments: Unique, 4-lobed pods. Mild pungency.

▼ ▼ ▼ ▼ ▼ ▼ ▼ ▼ ▼ ▼

USDA # none

Botanical name: *Capsicum baccatum* cv. 'Peruvian Dark Red'

Common name: Peruvian dark red ají

Location: Peru

Seed source: Seed Savers Exchange

Pod length: 3.5 in.

Pod width: 1.25 in.

Immature color: green

Mature color: yellow

Comments: Note the unusual apex of the pod. Medium heat.

USDA # none

Botanical name: *Capsicum baccatum* cv. 'Peru Yellow'

Common names: Peru yellow ají; ají limón

Location: Peru

Seed source: Enchanted Seeds, Seed Savers Exchange

Pod length: 1.5 in.

Pod width: .5 in.

Immature color: green

Mature color: yellow

Comments: Flower white with spots. Hot fruits that grow horizontally and sometimes erect. Lemony flavor overtones. Grows well in pots.

USDA # none

Botanical name: *Capsicum baccatum* cv. 'Kovinchu'

Common name: ají kovinchu

Location: Peru

Seed source: Seed Savers Exchange

Pod length: 4 in.

Pod width: .5 in.

Immature color: green

Mature color: red

Comments: Thin-walled fruits. Medium heat. Prolific.

▼ ▼ ▼ ▼ ▼ ▼ ▼ ▼ ▼ ▼ ▼

USDA # none

Botanical name: *Capsicum baccatum* cv. 'Cochabamba'

Common name: ají cochabamba

Location: Bolivia

Seed source: Seed Savers Exchange

Pod length: 4 in.

Pod width: .75 in.

Immature color: green

Mature color: red

Comments: Some pods measure only 2 inches long. Medium heat.

▼ ▼ ▼ ▼ ▼ ▼ ▼ ▼ ▼ ▼ ▼

USDA # none

Botanical name: *Capsicum baccatum* cv. 'Serranito'

Common name: ají serranito

Location: Peru

Seed source: Seed Savers Exchange

Pod length: 2.5 in.

Pod width: .35 in.

Immature color: green

Mature color: red

Comments: Medium heat. Prolific.

▼ ▼ ▼ ▼ ▼ ▼ ▼ ▼ ▼ ▼

USDA # none

Botanical name: *Capsicum baccatum* cv. 'Escabeche'

Common name: ají escabeche

Location: South America

Seed source: Seed Savers Exchange

Pod length: 5 in.

Pod width: 1 in.

Immature color: green

Mature color: orange-red

Comments: Medium heat. Tall. Vigorous plant.

▼ ▼ ▼ ▼ ▼ ▼ ▼ ▼ ▼ ▼

USDA # none

Botanical name: *Capsicum baccatum* cv. 'Ecuadoran Red'

Common name: Ecuadoran red ají

Location: Ecuador

Seed source: Seed Savers Exchange

Pod length: 2 in.

Pod width: .75 in.

Immature color: light green

Mature color: red

Comments: Sometimes called Ecuadoran light green. Prolific. Hot pods. Some pods up to 4 inches long.

▼ ▼ ▼ ▼ ▼ ▼ ▼ ▼ ▼ ▼

USDA #260566

Botanical name: *Capsicum baccatum* cv. 'Bolivian Long'

Common Name: Bolivian long ají

Location: Bolivia

Seed source: USDA

Pod length: 4 in.

Pod width: .5 in.

Immature color: green

Mature color: red

Comments: Thin-podded. Prolific pods; medium heat.

▼ ▼ ▼ ▼ ▼ ▼ ▼ ▼ ▼ ▼

USDA # none

Botanical name: *Capsicum baccatum* cv. 'Kellu-Uchu'

Common names: kellu-uchu, ají amarillo

Location: Peru

Seed source: Seed Savers Exchange

Pod length: 4.5 in.

Pod width: 2.25 in.

Immature color: green

Mature color: yellow

Comments: One of the most common Peruvian ajís; medium heat.

▼ ▼ ▼ ▼ ▼ ▼ ▼ ▼ ▼ ▼ ▼

USDA #439373

Botanical name: *Capsicum baccatum*

Common name: unknown

Location: Costa Rica

Seed source: USDA

Pod length: 1.75 in.

Pod width: .75 in.

Immature color: green

Mature color: orange

Comments: White flowers with yellow spots.

▼ ▼ ▼ ▼ ▼ ▼ ▼ ▼ ▼ ▼ ▼

USDA #321078

Botanical name: *Capsicum baccatum*

Common name: unknown

Location: Kenya

Seed source: USDA

Pod length: 3 in.

Pod width: .75 in.

Immature color: green

Mature color: red

Comments: Flower white with yellow spots.

▼ ▼ ▼ ▼ ▼ ▼ ▼ ▼ ▼ ▼ ▼

USDA #267729

Botanical name: *Capsicum baccatum*

Common name: hot pepper tree

Location: Guatemala

Seed source: USDA

Pod length: 3 in.

Pod width: .75 in.

Immature color: green

Mature color: red

Comments: White flower with yellow spots.

▼ ▼ ▼ ▼ ▼ ▼ ▼ ▼ ▼ ▼ ▼

USDA #497972

Botanical name: *Capsicum baccatum* cv. 'Dedo do Moca'

Common name: dedo do moca

Location: Brazil

Seed source: USDA

Pod length: 3. in.

Pod width: .5 in.

Immature color: green

Mature color: red

Comments: White flower with yellow spots.

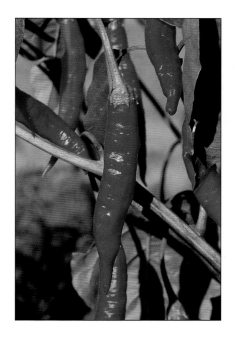

▼ ▼ ▼ ▼ ▼ ▼ ▼ ▼ ▼ ▼ ▼

USDA #441588

Botanical name: *Capsicum baccatum*

Common name: unknown

Location: Brazil

Seed source: USDA

Pod length: 2.5 in.

Pod width: .5 in.

Immature color: green

Mature color: reddish orange

Comments: Flower white with yellow spots.

▼ ▼ ▼ ▼ ▼ ▼ ▼ ▼ ▼ ▼ ▼

USDA #188803

Botanical name: *Capsicum baccatum* cv. 'Sil-a-Top'

Common name: sil-a-top pepper

Location: Philippines

Seed source: USDA

Pod length: 4 in.

Pod width: .5 in.

Immature color: yellow

Mature color: orange

Comments: White flower with yellow spots.

▼ ▼ ▼ ▼ ▼ ▼ ▼ ▼ ▼ ▼

USDA #281415

Botanical name: *Capsicum baccatum*

Common name: unknown

Location: Peru

Seed source: USDA

Pod length: 4 in.

Pod width: .75 in.

Immature color: yellow-green

Mature color: orange

Comments: Flower white with yellow spots.

▼ ▼ ▼ ▼ ▼ ▼ ▼ ▼ ▼ ▼

USDA #199506

Botanical name: *Capsicum baccatum*

Common name: unknown

Location: Guyana

Seed source: USDA

Pod length: 3.5 in.

Pod width: .75 in.

Immature color: green

Mature color: yellow

Comments: Flower white with yellow spots.

▼ ▼ ▼ ▼ ▼ ▼ ▼ ▼ ▼ ▼ ▼

USDA #281340

Botanical name: *Capsicum baccatum*

Common name: unknown

Location: Ecuador

Seed source: USDA

Pod length: 3.5 in.

Pod width: .5 in.

Immature color: yellow

Mature color: red

Comments: Flower white with yellow spots.

▼ ▼ ▼ ▼ ▼ ▼ ▼ ▼ ▼ ▼ ▼

USDA # none

Botanical name: *Capsicum baccatum* cv. 'Ají Amarillo'

Common name: ají amarillo

Location: Andes region

Seed source: Enchanted Seeds

Pod length: 2.25 in.

Pod width: .5 in.

Immature color: white

Mature color: yellow

Comments: White flower with yellow spots. A common variety.

▼ ▼ ▼ ▼ ▼ ▼ ▼ ▼ ▼ ▼

USDA # none

Botanical name: *Capsicum baccatum* cv. 'White Wax'

Common name: white wax ají

Location: South America

Seed source: The Pepper Gal

Pod length: 3.5 in.

Pod width: .75 in.

Immature color: white

Mature color: reddish orange

Comments: Flower white with yellow spots.

▲ ▲ ▲ ▲ ▲ ▲ ▲

Onza chiles in market in Oaxaca

▼ ▼ ▼ ▼ ▼ ▼ ▼

The Hottest of Them All:
Capsicum chinense

THIS ENTIRE SPECIES IS OFTEN REFERRED to as habanero, but that appellation is a misnomer because there are hundreds of varieties within this species, and the name habanero refers to a specific pod type from the Yucatán Peninsula of Mexico and Belize.

The Amazon Basin was the center of origin for the C. *chinense* species, famous for having the hottest peppers in the world. The oldest known C. *chinense* ever found was the 6,500-year-old intact pod found in Guitarrero Cave in Peru.

Bernabe Cobo, a naturalist who traveled throughout South America during the early seventeenth century, was probably the first European to study the C. *chinense* species. He estimated that there were at least forty different varieties, "some as large as limes or large plums; others, as small as pine nuts or even grains of wheat, and between the two extremes are many different sizes. No less variety is found in color...and the same difference is found in form and shape."

The species was first listed botanically in 1768 in *A Gardener's Dictionary* by Phillip Miller, who identified it as *Capsicum angulofum*, a West Indian pepper with wrinkled leaves and a bonnet shape. The species was then misnamed *Capsicum chinense* in 1776 by Nikolaus von Jacquin, a Dutch physician who collected plants in the Caribbean for Emperor Francis I from 1754 to 1759. Jacquin, who first described the species as "chinense" in his work, *Hortus botanicus vindobonensis*, wrote, mysteriously, "I have taken the plant's name from its homeland."

Why would Jacquin write that a plant native to the West Indies

Pod variations in _C. chinense_

was from China? Jacquin had never collected plants in China, and considering the fact that the first Chinese laborers to the West Indies would not arrive in Cuba until the early 1800s, it is unlikely that Jacquin crossed paths with any suspected Chinese "importers" of the species. It is likely that this pepper mystery will never be solved, so we are stuck with a totally inaccurate species name of a supposedly Chinese pepper that's not from China. And so far, no taxonomist has gone out on a limb to correct this obvious error.

C. _chinense_ is the most important cultivated pepper east of the Andes in South America. There is a great diversity of pod shape, and their heat levels range from zero to more than 500,000 Scoville heat units. At some point in time, Native Americans transferred the C. _chinense_ from the Amazon Basin into the Caribbean.

The seeds were carried and cultivated by Native Americans, and the C. _chinense_ species hopped, skipped, and jumped around the West Indies, forming—seemingly on each island—specifically adapted pod types that are called land races of the species. These land races were given local names in the various islands and countries, although the terms Scotch bonnet, goat pepper, and habanero are also used generically throughout the region.

In the eastern Caribbean, habanero relatives are called Congo peppers in Trinidad and booney or bonney peppers in Barbados. In the

C. chinense **harvest**

French Caribbean islands of Martinque and Guadeloupe, "le derriere de Madame Jacques" describes the hot peppers, and in Haiti, "piment bouc," or goat pepper. In the western Caribbean are the familiar Jamaican Scotch bonnets, Puerto Rican rocotillos, and the Cuban *cachucha* (cap) peppers.

These land races with the colorful names became the dominant spicy element in the food of the Caribbean.

C. chinense varieties range between 1 and 4.5 feet tall, depending on environmental factors. Some perennial varieties have grown as tall as 8 feet in tropical climates, but the average height in U.S. gardens is about 2 feet. It has multiple stems and an erect habit. The leaves are pale to medium green, are large and wrinkled, and reach up to 6 inches long and 4 inches wide.

The flowers have white or green corollas and purple anthers. The plant sets 2 to 6 fruits per node. The pods of the *C. chinense* species vary enormously in size and shape, ranging from chiltepín-sized berries .25 inch in diameter to wrinkled and elongated pods up to 5 inches long. The familar habaneros are pendant, lantern shaped, and some are pointed at the end. Caribbean chineses are often flattened at the end and resemble a tam, or bonnet. Often the blossom ends of these pods are inverted. The pods are usually green at immaturity and usually mature to red, orange, yellow, or white. Brown mature pods have also been described. *C. chinense* pods are characterized by a distinctive, fruity aroma that is often described as apricot-like. Interestingly enough, that aroma is present regardless of the variety, heat level, or size of the pod.

The heat level of the *C. chinense* species has been the subject of much discussion. Phrases like "hottest pepper in the world" and "a thousand times hotter than a jalapeño" have been bandied about for years, but they don't really tell the story. In actuality, the species does have nonpungent varieties, just like the bell peppers of the *C. annuum* species. Thus the heat scale ranges from zero to 577,000 Scoville units, the hottest *C. chinense* ever measured. In terms of the average number of Scoville heat units, a habanero, for example, is about fifty times hotter than a jalapeño—as measured by machines, not the human mouth. Because humans have varying numbers of taste buds, reaction can vary enormously from person to person.

Another member of the *C. chinense* species that is commonly used, especially in the eastern Caribbean, is the seasoning pepper. It is a medium-hot, elongated pepper that is used in quantity for seasoning pastes in Trinidad, Barbados, Antigua, St. Lucia, and other islands.

In the Yucatán Peninsula the *C. chinense* is called habanero, which means "from Havana," hinting of a transference to Mexico from the Caribbean. It long has been rumored that habaneros no longer grow in Cuba, but pepper aficionado Richard Rice sent us seeds in 1990 given to him by Cuban refugees. The seeds did indeed produce habaneros, proving they are still grown in Cuba today. The species was transferred to Africa during the colonization of Brazil or during the later traffic in slaves, and today there are many *C. chinense* varieties in Africa.

Today, habaneros are grown commercially in the Yucatán Peninsula of Mexico, where about 1500 tons a year are harvested. They are cultivated to a lesser extent in Belize, and there are small commercial fields of other *C. chinense* varieties in Jamaica, Trinidad, and to a limited extent on other islands, such as the Bahamas. In Costa Rica, a cultivar of *C. chinense* called 'Rica Red,' developed by Stuart Jeffrey and Cody Jordan of Quetzál Foods, is grown commercially, with about 200 acres under cultivation in 1992. In the United States, there are two significant commercial growing operations: one in California and the other in the Texas Hill Country. The datil pepper, a *C. chinese* variety grown for about 300 years in St. Augustine, Florida, is processed into sauces and jellies. Although Mexican varieties have been developed and named, none are commercially available to home gardeners. In the United States, most commercial habanero seeds are generic.

Interestingly enough, in the Amazon region of Brazil, mildly pungent *C. chinense* varieties have been crossed with bell peppers to produce sweet hybrids that are more disease resistant than annuums under hot and humid conditions. S. S. Cheng, the researcher responsible for the experiment, notes: "The advantages of *C. chinense* cultivation are the longer harvest periods, no pesticide application requirement, and low production cost. A breeding program is under way to transfer fruit quality from *C. annuum* to *C. chinense.*"

The seeds tend to take a long time to germinate. The *C. chinense*, being tropical plants, do best in areas with high humidity and warm nights. They are slow growing, especially in the Southwest, with a growing period of 80 to 120 days or more. Gardening writer Rosalind Creasy reports she has good success with habaneros in Northern California. The yield varies enormously according to how well the particular plants adapt to the local environment; we have grown stunted plants with as few as 10 pods, and large, bushy plants with 50 or more pods.

The *C. chinense* pods are used fresh in salsas, and are commonly used to make very hot, liquid sauces when combined with carrots and onions. They can be dried and ground into powder, but be sure to wear a protective mask.

For more information on *C. chinense*, see *The Habanero Cookbook*, by Dave DeWitt and Nancy Gerlach (Berkeley, CA: Ten Speed Press, 1995.)

▼ ▼ ▼ ▼ ▼ ▼ ▼ ▼ ▼ ▼ ▼

USDA # none

Botanical name: *Capsicum chinense*

Common names: yellow bird's eye, Brazilian bird pepper

Location: Brazil

Seed source: Seed Savers Exchange

Pod length: .25 in.

Pod width: .25 in.

Immature color: green

Mature color: yellow

Comments: Extremely hot; characteristic fruity *C. chinense* aroma. Probably a wild form.

▼ ▼ ▼ ▼ ▼ ▼ ▼ ▼ ▼ ▼ ▼

USDA #260501

Botanical name: *Capsicum chinense*

Common name: charapita

Location: Peru

Seed source: USDA

Pod length: .5 in.

Pod width: .25 in.

Immature color: green

Mature color: orange

Comments: Flower color is green. Another wild form.

▼ ▼ ▼ ▼ ▼ ▼ ▼ ▼ ▼ ▼ ▼

USDA #281421

Botanical name: *Capsicum chinense*

Common name: siling labuyo

Location: Philippines

Seed source: USDA

Pod length: .5 in.

Pod width: .25 in.

Immature color: green

Mature color: red

Comments: Sometimes thought to be *frutescens.* Very pungent.

▼ ▼ ▼ ▼ ▼ ▼ ▼ ▼ ▼ ▼ ▼

USDA #281353

Botanical name: *Capsicum chinense*

Common name: unknown

Location: Pacific Island Trust

Seed source: USDA

Pod length: 1 in.

Pod width: .25 in.

Immature color: green

Mature color: red

Comments: Flower is green.

▼ ▼ ▼ ▼ ▼ ▼ ▼ ▼ ▼ ▼ ▼

USDA #281314

Botanical name: *Capsicum chinense*

Common name: unknown

Location: Guyana

Seed source: USDA

Pod length: 1 in.

Pod width: .5 in.

Immature color: green or purple

Mature color: red

Comments: Very pungent.

▼ ▼ ▼ ▼ ▼ ▼ ▼ ▼ ▼ ▼ ▼

USDA #441715

Botanical name: *Capsicum chinense*

Common name: unknown

Location: Brazil

Seed source: USDA

Pod length: .5 in.

Pod width: .5 in.

Immature color: green

Mature color: red

Comments: Very pungent.

▼ ▼ ▼ ▼ ▼ ▼ ▼ ▼ ▼ ▼ ▼

USDA #281440

Botanical name: *Capsicum chinense*

Common name: unknown

Location: Venezuela

Seed source: USDA

Pod length: 1. in.

Pod width: .75 in.

Immature color: green

Mature color: yellow

Comments: Very pungent.

▼ ▼ ▼ ▼ ▼ ▼ ▼ ▼ ▼ ▼ ▼

USDA #224446

Botanical name: *Capsicum chinense*

Common name: unknown

Location: Costa Rica

Seed source: USDA

Pod length: 1 in.

Pod width: .75 in.

Immature color: yellow

Mature color: red

Comments: Very pungent. Pods are erect.

▼ ▼ ▼ ▼ ▼ ▼ ▼ ▼ ▼ ▼

USDA # none

Botanical name: *Capsicum chinense* cv. 'Cheira Bell'

Common name: cheira bell

Location: Brazil

Seed source: Seed Savers Exchange

Pod length: .75 in.

Pod width: .5 in.

Immature color: green-purple

Mature color: red

Comments: Medium pungency.

▼ ▼ ▼ ▼ ▼ ▼ ▼ ▼ ▼ ▼

USDA #238047

Botanical name: *Capsicum chinense*

Common name: unknown

Location: Guyana

Seed source: USDA

Pod length: 1 in.

Pod width: .25 in.

Immature color: green, yellow

Mature color: red

Comments: Very pungent.

▼ ▼ ▼ ▼ ▼ ▼ ▼ ▼ ▼ ▼

USDA #543208

Botanical name: *Capsicum chinense*

Common name: unknown

Location: Bolivia

Seed source: USDA

Pod length: .75 in.

Pod width: .5 in.

Immature color: green

Mature color: red

Comments: Very pungent.

▼ ▼ ▼ ▼ ▼ ▼ ▼ ▼ ▼ ▼

USDA #543205

Botanical name: *Capsicum chinense*

Common name: unknown

Location: Bolivia

Seed source: USDA

Pod length: .5 in.

Pod width: .5 in.

Immature color: yellow

Mature color: red

Comments: Very pungent.

▼ ▼ ▼ ▼ ▼ ▼ ▼ ▼ ▼ ▼

USDA #238046

Botanical name: *Capsicum chinense*

Common name: unknown

Location: Guyana

Seed source: USDA

Pod length: .5 in.

Pod width: .5 in.

Immature color: green-purple

Mature color: red

Comments: Flower is green. Very pungent.

▼ ▼ ▼ ▼ ▼ ▼ ▼ ▼ ▼ ▼

USDA #441657

Botanical name: *Capsicum chinense*

Common name: unknown

Location: Brazil

Seed source: USDA

Pod length: .5 in.

Pod width: .25 in.

Immature color: green

Mature color: yellow

Comments: Very pungent.

▼ ▼ ▼ ▼ ▼ ▼ ▼ ▼ ▼ ▼ ▼

USDA #257138

Botanical name: *Capsicum chinense*

Common name: unknown

Location: Ecuador

Seed source: USDA

Pod length: 1.25 in.

Pod width: .5 in.

Immature color: light green

Mature color: red

Comments: Very pungent.

▼ ▼ ▼ ▼ ▼ ▼ ▼ ▼ ▼ ▼ ▼

USDA #370005

Botanical name: *Capsicum chinense*

Common name: unknown

Location: India

Seed source: USDA

Pod length: 1.5 in.

Pod width: .5 in.

Immature color: yellow

Mature color: red

Comments: Closely resembles *C. frutescens.*

▼ ▼ ▼ ▼ ▼ ▼ ▼ ▼ ▼ ▼ ▼

USDA #497985

Botanical name: *Capsicum chinense*

Common name: cumari o passarinho

Location: Brazil

Seed source: USDA

Pod length: 1.25 in.

Pod width: .5 in.

Immature color: green

Mature color: orange

Comments: Very pungent.

▼ ▼ ▼ ▼ ▼ ▼ ▼ ▼ ▼ ▼ ▼

USDA #152452

Botanical name: *Capsicum chinense*

Common name: unknown

Location: Brazil

Seed source: USDA

Pod length: .5 in.

Pod width: .5 in.

Immature color: green

Mature color: yellow

Comments: Very pungent.

▼ ▼ ▼ ▼ ▼ ▼ ▼ ▼ ▼ ▼ ▼

USDA # none

Botanical name: *Capsicum chinense* cv. 'Datil'

Common name: datil pepper

Location: St. Augustine, Florida

Seed source: The Pepper Gal

Pod length: 3.25 in.

Pod width: .75 in.

Immature color: green

Mature color: yellow or red

Comments: Long culivated near St. Augustine, this variety is used in hot sauces and other spicy products.

▼ ▼ ▼ ▼ ▼ ▼ ▼ ▼ ▼ ▼ ▼

USDA # none

Botanical name: *Capsicum chinense* cv. 'Habanero'

Common name: habanero chile

Location: Yucatán Peninsula, Mexico, and Belize

Seed sources: Enchanted Seeds, Shepherd's

Pod length: 2.5 in.

Pod width: 1 in.

Immature color: green

Mature color: orange

Comments: This is the familiar, generic orange habanero. It is usually extremely hot and is used in sauces and seafood dishes.

▼ ▼ ▼ ▼ ▼ ▼ ▼ ▼ ▼ ▼ ▼

USDA #224443

Botanical name: *Capsicum chinense* cv. 'Bolivian Red'

Common name: Bolivian red

Location: Bolivia

Seed source: Seed Savers Exchange

Pod length: 2 in.

Pod Width: 1 in.

Immature color: green

Mature color: red

Comments: Prolific; very pungent. Grows well in pots.

▼ ▼ ▼ ▼ ▼ ▼ ▼ ▼ ▼ ▼ ▼

USDA # none

Botanical name: *Capsicum chinense* cv. 'Chombo'

Common name: aji chombo

Location: Panama

Seed source: Seed Savers Exchange

Pod length: 2.25 in.

Pod width: 1 in.

Immature color: green

Mature color: red

Comments: Very pungent; used in hot sauces. Grows well in pots.

▼ ▼ ▼ ▼ ▼ ▼ ▼ ▼ ▼ ▼ ▼

USDA # none

Botanical name: *Capsicum chinense* cv. 'Fatalii'

Common name: fatalii pepper

Location: Central African Republic

Seed source: Old Southwest Trading Company

Pod length: 3 in.

Pod width: 1.5 in.

Immature color: pale green

Mature color: yellow

Comments: Extremely pungent, prolific. Thin walled. Grows well in pots.

▼ ▼ ▼ ▼ ▼ ▼ ▼ ▼ ▼ ▼

USDA # none

Botanical name: *Capsicum chinense* cv. 'Seasoning Pepper'

Common name: Trinidad seasoning pepper

Location: Trinidad and Tobago

Seed source: Old Southwest Trading Company

Pod length: 3.5 in.

Pod width: 1.25 in.

Immature color: green

Mature color: red

Comments: A mild *C. chinense* used in seasoning pastes; also called pimiento or long pimiento. Grows well in pots.

▼ ▼ ▼ ▼ ▼ ▼ ▼ ▼ ▼ ▼ ▼

USDA #238051

Botanical name: *Capsicum chinense* cv. 'Shiny Red'

Common name: Peruvian shiny red

Location: Peru

Seed source: Seed Savers Exchange

Pod length: 1 in.

Pod width: .75 in.

Immature color: green

Mature color: red

Comments: Also known as chinchi-uchu. Very pungent. Grows well in pots.

▼ ▼ ▼ ▼ ▼ ▼ ▼ ▼ ▼ ▼ ▼

USDA #238052

Botanical name: *Capsicum chinense* cv. 'Peruvian Golden'

Common name: Peruvian golden

Location: Peru

Seed source: Seed Savers Exchange

Pod length: 1 in.

Pod width: .75 in.

Immature color: green

Mature color: yellow

Comments: Profilic, very pungent. Grows well in pots.

▼ ▼ ▼ ▼ ▼ ▼ ▼ ▼ ▼ ▼ ▼

USDA # none

Botanical name: *Capsicum chinense* cv. 'Round Pepper'

Common name: round pepper

Location: Trinidad and Tobago

Seed source: collected in Port of Spain market

Pod length: 1.5 in.

Pod width: 2 in.

Immature color: green orange

Mature color: red

Comments: Very colorful as it matures. Medium heat. May be the same as Congo pepper. Grows well in pots.

▼ ▼ ▼ ▼ ▼ ▼ ▼ ▼ ▼ ▼ ▼

USDA # none

Botanical name: *Capsicum chinense* cv. 'Congo'

Common name: Congo pepper

Location: Trinidad and Tobago

Seed source: Old Southwest Trading Company

Pod length: 2.5 in.

Pod width: 3 in.

Immature color: green

Mature color: red

Comments: Very large, extremely pungent. Main pepper of eastern Caribbean, used in hot sauces. Grows well in pots.

▼ ▼ ▼ ▼ ▼ ▼ ▼ ▼ ▼ ▼ ▼

USDA # none

Botanical name: *Capsicum chinense* cv. 'Rica Red'

Common name: Rica red habanero

Location: Costa Rica

Seed source: Old Southwest Trading Co.

Pod length: 2.5 in.

Pod width: 1.5 in.

Immature color: green

Mature color: red

Comments: Developed from cross-breeding Costa Rican red habaneros; used to make pepper mash for hot sauces. Very pungent.

▼ ▼ ▼ ▼ ▼ ▼ ▼ ▼ ▼ ▼ ▼

USDA # none

Botanical name: *Capsicum chinense* cv. 'Antiqua Seasoning'

Common name: Antigua seasoning pepper

Location: Antigua, West Indies

Seed source: collected in Antigua; try Seed Savers Exchange

Pod length: 1.25 in.

Pod width: .75 in.

Immature color: green

Mature color: red

Comments: Medium heat, used in seasoning pastes.

▼ ▼ ▼ ▼ ▼ ▼ ▼ ▼ ▼ ▼ ▼

USDA # none

Botanical name: *Capsicum chinense* cv. 'Rocotillo'

Common name: Cayman rocotillo

Locations: Grand Cayman, British West Indies

Seed source: collected in market in Grand Cayman

Pod length: .5 in.

Pod width: .75 in.

Immature color: green

Mature color: yellow

Comments: A small, mild pod from the Cayman Islands; other rocotillos are larger.

▼ ▼ ▼ ▼ ▼ ▼ ▼ ▼ ▼ ▼ ▼

USDA # none

Botanical name: *Capsicum chinense* cv. 'Yaquitania'

Common name: ají yaquitania

Location: Brazil

Seed source: Seed Savers Exchange

Pod length: .75 in.

Pod width: .5 in.

Immature color: green

Mature color: orange

Comments: Hot pods, small but prolific. Grows well in pots, winters over nicely. This specimen is from a plant 3 years old.

▼ ▼ ▼ ▼ ▼ ▼ ▼ ▼ ▼ ▼ ▼

USDA # none

Botanical name: *Capsicum chinense* cv. 'Scotch bonnet'

Common names: Scotch bonnet, Scot's bonnet

Location: Jamaica

Seed source: Seed Savers Exchange

Pod length: 1.5 in.

Pod width: 1 in.

Immature color: green

Mature color: yellow or red

Comments: Sometimes has smoother pods. Very pungent.

▼ ▼ ▼ ▼ ▼ ▼ ▼ ▼ ▼ ▼ ▼

USDA #543207

Botanical name: *Capsicum chinense*

Common name: unknown

Location: Bolivia

Seed source: USDA

Pod length: 1 in.

Pod width: 1.75 in.

Immature color: yellow

Mature color: red

Comments: Very pungent.

▼ ▼ ▼ ▼ ▼ ▼ ▼ ▼ ▼ ▼

USDA # 543193

Botanical name: *Capsicum chinense*

Common name: unknown

Location: Bolivia

Seed source: USDA

Pod length: 1 in.

Pod width: .75 in.

Immature color: green

Mature color: orange

Comments: Flower color is green. Very pungent.

▼ ▼ ▼ ▼ ▼ ▼ ▼ ▼ ▼ ▼

USDA #543196

Botanical name: *Capsicum chinense*

Common name: unknown

Location: Bolivia

Seed source: USDA

Pod length: 2.25 in.

Pod width: 1 in.

Immature color: green

Mature color: red or orange

Comments: Very pungent.

▼ ▼ ▼ ▼ ▼ ▼ ▼ ▼ ▼ ▼ ▼

USDA #215731

Botanical name: *Capsicum chinense*

Common name: unknown

Location: Peru

Seed source: USDA

Pod length: 1.25 in.

Pod width: .75 in.

Immature color: green

Mature color: red

Comments: Flower is green. Very pungent.

▼ ▼ ▼ ▼ ▼ ▼ ▼ ▼ ▼ ▼ ▼

USDA # none

Botanical name: *Capsicum chinense* cv. 'Rocotillo'

Common name: rocotillo pepper

Location: West Indies

Seed source: Seed Savers Exchange

Pod length: 1.25 in.

Pod width: 1.75 in.

Immature color: light green

Mature color: red

Comments: Larger than the Cayman rocotillo; mild.

▼ ▼ ▼ ▼ ▼ ▼ ▼ ▼ ▼ ▼ ▼

USDA #215733

Botanical name: *Capsicum chinense*

Common name: unknown

Location: Peru

Seed source: USDA

Pod length: 1.25 in.

Pod width: 1.25 in.

Immature color: green

Mature color: orange

Comments: Flower is green. Very pungent.

▼ ▼ ▼ ▼ ▼ ▼ ▼ ▼ ▼ ▼ ▼

USDA #281424

Botanical name: *Capsicum chinense* cv. 'Red Squash'

Common name: red squash pepper

Location: Puerto Rico

Seed source: USDA

Pod length: 1.25 in.

Pod width: 1.25 in.

Immature color: green

Mature color: red

Comments: Flower color is green. Not to be confused with the 'Red Squash' that is an *annuum*. Medium pungency.

▼ ▼ ▼ ▼ ▼ ▼ ▼ ▼ ▼ ▼ ▼

USDA #487452

Botanical name: *Capsicum chinense*

Common name: unknown

Location: Venezuela

Seed source: USDA

Pod length: 1 in.

Pod width: .5 in.

Immature color: green

Mature color: red

Comments: Very pungent.

▼ ▼ ▼ ▼ ▼ ▼ ▼ ▼ ▼ ▼ ▼

USDA #257071

Botanical name: *Capsicum chinense*

Common name: unknown

Location: Colombia

Seed source: USDA

Pod length: 1.5 in.

Pod width: .5 in.

Immature color: green

Mature color: orange

Comments: Note elongated, pendant pod. Very pungent.

▼ ▼ ▼ ▼ ▼ ▼ ▼ ▼ ▼ ▼

USDA #260464

Botanical name: *Capsicum chinense*

Common name: unknown

Location: Argentina

Seed source: USDA

Pod length: 1.5 in.

Pod width: .5 in.

Immature color: green

Mature color: red

Comments: Very pungent.

▼ ▼ ▼ ▼ ▼ ▼ ▼ ▼ ▼ ▼

USDA # none

Botanical name: *Capsicum chinense* cv. 'Red Savina'

Common name: red savina habanero

Location: California, USA

Seed source: Shepherd's Garden Seeds

Pod length: 2 in.

Pod width: 1 in.

Immature color: green

Mature color: red

Comments: The first habanero to receive USDA plant-protection certificate. This is generally regarded as the most pungent chile ever measured, at 577,000 Scoville heat units.

▼ ▼ ▼ ▼ ▼ ▼ ▼ ▼ ▼ ▼ ▼

USDA #159248

Botanical name: *Capsicum chinense*

Common name: unknown

Location: USA

Seed source: USDA

Pod length: 1.25 in.

Pod width: .75 in.

Immature color: green

Mature color: ivory

Comments: Flower is green; this variety has been a valuable source of virus resistance.

▼ ▼ ▼ ▼ ▼ ▼ ▼ ▼ ▼ ▼ ▼

USDA #291429

Botanical name: *Capsicum chinense*

Common name: unknown

Location: Surinam

Seed source: USDA

Pod length: 1.5 in.

Pod width: .75 in.

Immature color: light green

Mature color: salmon

Comments: Flower color is green. Very pungent.

▼ ▼ ▼ ▼ ▼ ▼ ▼ ▼ ▼ ▼ ▼

USDA # none

Botanical name: *Capsicum chinense* cv. 'Chocolate Habanero'

Common name: chocolate habanero

Location: West Indies

Seed source: The Pepper Gal

Pod length: 2.5 in.

Pod width: 1.5 in.

Immature color: green

Mature color: brown

Comments: Flower color is green. Very pungent.

▼ ▼ ▼ ▼ ▼ ▼ ▼ ▼ ▼ ▼

USDA #224448

Botanical name: *Capsicum chinense* cv. 'Yellow Habanero'

Common name: yellow habanero

Location: Costa Rica

Seed source: USDA

Pod length: 1.75 in.

Pod width: 1.5 in.

Immature color: yellow-green

Mature color: yellow

Comments: Very pungent.

▼ ▼ ▼ ▼ ▼ ▼ ▼ ▼ ▼ ▼ ▼

USDA #543181

Botanical name: *Capsicum chinense*

Common name: unknown

Location: Bolivia

Seed source: USDA

Pod length: 1.5 in.

Pod width: 1 in.

Immature color: green

Mature color: orange

Comments: Very pungent.

▼ ▼ ▼ ▼ ▼ ▼ ▼ ▼ ▼ ▼ ▼

USDA #224424

Botanical name: *Capsicum chinense*

Common name: unknown

Location: Costa Rica

Seed source: USDA

Pod length: 1.75 in.

Pod width: 1 in.

Immature color: green

Mature color: orange

Comments: Flower is green. Very pungent. Note the multiple fruits set at a single stem.

▼ ▼ ▼ ▼ ▼ ▼ ▼ ▼ ▼ ▼

USDA #438532

Botanical name: *Capsicum chinense* cv. 'Habanero Rojo'

Common name: red habanero

Location: Belize

Seed source: USDA

Pod length: 1.75 in.

Pod width: 1 in.

Immature color: green

Mature color: red

Comments: Used to make hot sauce in Belize. Very pungent.

▼ ▼ ▼ ▼ ▼ ▼ ▼ ▼ ▼ ▼

USDA #543202

Botanical name: *Capsicum chinense* cv. 'Ají Dulce'

Common names: ají dulce, sweet pepper

Location: Bolivia

Seed source: USDA

Pod length: 1.5 in.

Pod width: 1 in.

Immature color: light green

Mature color: salmon

Comments: Flower color is green; this ají is *C. chinense*, not *baccatum*. A mild *chinense*, one of the few.

▼ ▼ ▼ ▼ ▼ ▼ ▼ ▼ ▼ ▼ ▼

USDA #257176

Botanical name: *Capsicum chinense*

Common name: unknown

Location: Peru

Seed source: USDA

Pod length: 1.5 in.

Pod width: 1 in.

Immature color: green

Mature color: yellow

Comments: Very pungent.

▼ ▼ ▼ ▼ ▼ ▼ ▼ ▼ ▼ ▼ ▼

USDA #560943

Botanical name: *Capsicum chinense*

Common name: unknown

Location: Bolivia

Seed source: USDA

Pod length: 1.5 in.

Pod width: 1 in.

Immature color: green

Mature color: red

Comments: Very pungent.

▼ ▼ ▼ ▼ ▼ ▼ ▼ ▼ ▼ ▼ ▼

USDA #152222

Botanical name: *Capsicum chinense*

Common name: unknown

Location: Peru

Seed source: USDA

Pod length: 1.5 in.

Pod width: 1 in.

Immature color: green

Mature color: yellow

Comments: Very pungent. Waxy skin.

▼ ▼ ▼ ▼ ▼ ▼ ▼ ▼ ▼ ▼ ▼

USDA #257132

Botanical name: *Capsicum chinense*

Common name: unknown

Location: Ecuador

Seed source: USDA

Pod length: 2 in.

Pod width: .75 in.

Immature color: green

Mature color: orange

Comments: Flower is green. Very pungent.

▼ ▼ ▼ ▼ ▼ ▼ ▼ ▼ ▼ ▼

USDA # none

Botanical name: *Capsicum chinense* cv. 'AZR'

Common name: AZR

Location: India

Seed source: Redwood City Seed Co.

Pod length: 2 in.

Pod width: .5 in.

Immature color: green

Mature color: red

Comments: Flower color is green.

▼ ▼ ▼ ▼ ▼ ▼ ▼ ▼ ▼ ▼

USDA #152225

Botanical name: *Capsicum chinense*

Common name: unknown

Location: Peru

Seed source: USDA

Pod length: 1.5 in.

Pod width: .5 in.

Immature color: green, purple

Mature color: red

Comments: Flower green. Very pungent.

▼ ▼ ▼ ▼ ▼ ▼ ▼ ▼ ▼ ▼

USDA # none

Botanical name: *Capsicum chinense* cv. 'Ají Brown'

Common name: Ají brown

Location: Peru

Seed source: Enchanted Seeds

Pod length: 2.75 in.

Pod width: 1 in.

Immature color: green

Mature color: brown

Comments: A *C. chinense* species even though called ají. Medium pungency.

▼ ▼ ▼ ▼ ▼ ▼ ▼ ▼ ▼ ▼

USDA #281417

Botanical name: *Capsicum chinense*

Common name: unknown

Location: Philippines

Seed source: USDA

Pod length: 4 in.

Pod width: .5 in.

Immature color: green

Mature color: red

Comments: Note elongated pod. Medium pungency.

▼ ▼ ▼ ▼ ▼ ▼ ▼ ▼ ▼ ▼ ▼

USDA #257045

Botanical name: *Capsicum chinense*

Common name: unknown

Location: Colombia

Seed source: USDA

Pod length: 2.25 in.

Pod width: .5 in.

Immature color: green

Mature color: red

Comments: Note elongated pod. Medium pungency.

▼ ▼ ▼ ▼ ▼ ▼ ▼ ▼ ▼ ▼ ▼

USDA #224447

Botanical name: *Capsicum chinense*

Common name: unknown

Location: Costa Rica

Seed source: USDA

Pod length: 1.25 in.

Pod width: 1.25 in.

Immature color: yellow, purple

Mature color: red

Comments: Flower green; note elongated pod. Medium pungency.

▼ ▼ ▼ ▼ ▼ ▼ ▼ ▼ ▼ ▼ ▼

USDA #194879

Botanical name: *Capsicum chinense* cv. 'Pinched Nose'

Common name: pinched nose pepper

Location: Guyana

Seed source: USDA

Pod length: 3.25 in.

Pod width: .5 in.

Immature color: green

Mature color: red

Comments: Note elongated pod. Medium pungency.

"Capsicum Kitten"—a chile vendor's pet in the the wholesale market, Bangkok, Thailand

A Plethora of Peppers:
Capsicum annuum

THE MOST LIKELY ANCESTOR OF THE COMMON *C. annuum* varieties grown in the garden today is the wild chiltepín (*C. annuum* var. *aviculare*). Botanists believe that these wild peppers are the closest surviving species to the earliest forms of annuums that developed in Bolivia and southern Brazil long before humans arrived in the Americas. The wild peppers spread all over South and Central America and up to what is now the United States border millennia before the domesticated varieties were developed. In fact, some botanists believe that the wild annuums have the widest distribution of any Western Hemisphere pepper variety, ranging from Peru to the Caribbean, Florida, Texas, and Louisiana and west to Arizona. (See Afterword, page 197.)

By the time the Spanish arrived in Mexico, Aztec plant breeders had already developed dozens of *C. annuum* varieties. According to historian Bernardino de Sahagún, who lived in Mexico in 1529, "hot green peppers, smoked peppers, water peppers, tree peppers, beetle peppers, and sharp-pointed red peppers" existed. Undoubtedly, these peppers were the precursors to the large number of *C. annuum* varieties found in Mexico today. Christopher Columbus took *C. annuum* seeds back to the Eastern Hemisphere, and they were planted extensively in the Portuguese and Spanish colonies in Africa, India, and Asia, resulting in even more diversification of the species.

C. annuum is the most extensively cultivated species in the world, both commercially and in home gardens. It is the principal species grown in Hungary, Spain, Netherlands, Turkey, Japan, India, Mexico, China, Korea, and the East Indies. Because the varieties cross-pollinate so easily, there are probably thousands of different varieties around the world. Many have similar common names, making identification difficult. In Mexico, for example, more than 200 common names for peppers are used—but only about fifteen C. *annuum* pod types are important cultivated crops.

Annuums used to be divided into two categories, sweet (or mild) peppers and hot (or chile) peppers. However, modern plant breeding removed that distinction because now hot bell varieties and sweet jalapeño and New Mexican varieties have been bred.

Another group of popular peppers is the ornamentals, or "Christmas peppers." They were called Christmas peppers because they were available at Christmas time, and they had green and red fruit colors. Nowadays, ornamental peppers and plants are available in more colors throughout the year. Although edible, ornamentals are grown primarily for their unusual pod shapes or for their dense and sometimes variegated foliage and colorful fruits. Ornamental peppers have all the colors of the rainbow, often displaying pods in four or five colors on the plant at the same time. Other ornamental types are used to make wreaths or other decorations. The subtle flavor associated with other peppers is missing in most ornamental peppers.

As mentioned in chapter one, these varieties are grouped roughly by pod shapes, moving from the smallest to the largest pods.

Chiltepíns drying, La Aurora, Sonora, Mexico

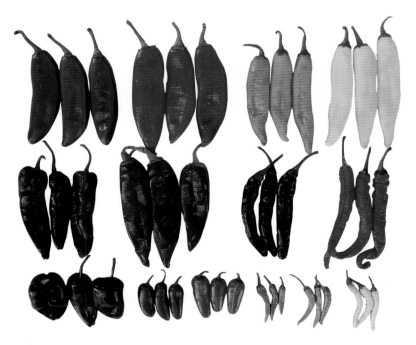

Pod variations in *C. annuum*

▼ ▼ ▼ ▼ ▼ ▼ ▼ ▼ ▼ ▼ ▼

USDA # none

Botanical name: *Capsicum annuum* var. *aviculare*

Common name: Sonoran chiltepín

Location: Sonora, Mexico

Seed sources: Seed Savers Exchange, Native Seeds/SEARCH

Pod length: .25 in.

Pod width: .25 in.

Immature color: green

Mature color: red

Comments: Grows wild throughout Mexico; extremely hot. See Afterword, page 197.

▼ ▼ ▼ ▼ ▼ ▼ ▼ ▼ ▼ ▼ ▼

USDA # none

Botanical name: *Capsicum annuum* var. *aviculare*

Common name: Arizona chiltepín

Location: Douglas, Arizona

Seed source: collected on location; try Seed Savers Exchange

Pod length: .5 in.

Pod width: .4 in.

Immature color: green

Mature color: red

Comments: Grows wild in southern Arizona; extremely pungent. Similar in habit to the Sonoran chiltepín.

▼ ▼ ▼ ▼ ▼ ▼ ▼ ▼ ▼ ▼ ▼

USDA # none

Botanical name: *Capsicum annuum* var. *aviculare*

Common name: chiltepín

Location: Sinaloa, Mexico

Seed source: Native Seeds/SEARCH

Pod length: .25 in.

Pod width: .25 in.

Immature color: green

Mature color: red

Comments: Most chiltepíns from northern Mexico are similar in appearance.

▼ ▼ ▼ ▼ ▼ ▼ ▼ ▼ ▼ ▼ ▼

USDA # none

Botanical name: *Capsicum annuum* var. *aviculare*

Common name: Trinidad bird pepper

Location: Northern Range, Trinidad

Seed source: collected on location; try Seed Savers Exchange

Pod length: .25 in.

Pod width: .25 in.

Immature color: green

Mature color: red

Comments: Many similar bird peppers grow on the Caribbean islands.

▼ ▼ ▼ ▼ ▼ ▼ ▼ ▼ ▼ ▼ ▼

USDA # none

Botanical name: *Capsicum annuum*

Common name: Bonaire bird pepper

Location: Bonaire, Netherlands Antilles

Seed source: collected on location; try Seed Savers Exchange

Pod length: .5 in.

Pod width: .25 in.

Immature color: green

Mature color: red

Comments: Collected by Nancy Gerlach. Erect habit, prolific. Extremely pungent.

▼ ▼ ▼ ▼ ▼ ▼ ▼ ▼ ▼ ▼ ▼

USDA #281299

Botanical name: *Capsicum annuum*

Common name: chile piquín

Location: Argentina

Seed source: USDA

Pod length: .75 in.

Pod width: .5 in.

Immature color: green

Mature color: red

Comments: Extremely pungent.

▼ ▼ ▼ ▼ ▼ ▼ ▼ ▼ ▼ ▼ ▼

USDA #566812

Botanical name: *Capsicum annuum*

Common name: chile piquín

Location: Mexico

Seed source: USDA

Pod length: .5 in.

Pod width: .25 in.

Immature color: green

Mature color: red-orange

Comments: Note the similarity to the previous pepper, despite the distances involved.

▼ ▼ ▼ ▼ ▼ ▼ ▼ ▼ ▼ ▼

USDA # none

Botanical name: *Capsicum annuum* cv. 'NuMex Bailey Piquín'

Common name: chile piquín

Location: New Mexico State University

Seed source: Enchanted Seeds

Pod length: .75 in.

Pod width: .25 in.

Immature color: green

Mature color: red

Comments: The first domesticated and machine-harvestable chile piquín.

▼ ▼ ▼ ▼ ▼ ▼ ▼ ▼ ▼ ▼ ▼

USDA # none

Botanical name: *Capsicum annuum* cv. 'Kalia'

Common names: Kalia pepper, ornamental

Location: USA

Seed source: The Pepper Gal

Pod length: .5 in.

Pod width: .25 in.

Immature color: green

Mature color: red

Comments: Vigorous, prolific.

▼ ▼ ▼ ▼ ▼ ▼ ▼ ▼ ▼ ▼ ▼

USDA # none

Botanical name: *Capsicum annuum* cv. 'Super Chili'

Common name: super chili

Location: USA

Seed source: Shepherd's Garden Seeds

Pod length: 1.5 in.

Pod width: .5 in.

Immature color: green

Mature color: red

Comments: A hybrid; compact plant growth, nice ornamental.

▼ ▼ ▼ ▼ ▼ ▼ ▼ ▼ ▼ ▼ ▼

USDA # none

Botanical name: *Capsicum annuum* cv. 'Santaka'

Common names: santaka, Asian hot

Location: Japan

Seed source: Seed Savers Exchange

Pod length: 2.5 in.

Pod width: .5 in.

Immature color: green

Mature color: red

Comments: Used in soups and stir-fries to provide pungency.

▼ ▼ ▼ ▼ ▼ ▼ ▼ ▼ ▼ ▼ ▼

USDA # none

Botanical name: *Capsicum annuum* cv. 'Tiny Samoa'

Common names: tiny Samoa, piquín

Location: Samoa

Seed source: The Pepper Gal

Pod length: .5 in.

Pod width: .25 in.

Immature color: green

Mature color: red

Comments: Shows the world-wide distribution of piquín types.

▼ ▼ ▼ ▼ ▼ ▼ ▼ ▼ ▼ ▼ ▼

USDA # none

Botanical name: *Capsicum annuum* cv. 'Thai Hot'

Common names: Thai hot, Asian hot

Location: Thailand

Seed source: Enchanted Seeds

Pod length: .75 in.

Pod width: .5 in.

Immature color: green

Mature color: red

Comments: A prolific and popular plant; usually an ornamental, but it is edible and quite hot.

▼ ▼ ▼ ▼ ▼ ▼ ▼ ▼ ▼ ▼ ▼

USDA #451762

Botanical name: *Capsicum annuum*

Common name: Israeli hot

Location: Israel

Seed source: USDA

Pod length: .75 in.

Pod width: .5 in.

Immature color: yellow

Mature color: red

Comments: A piquín type. Very pungent.

▼ ▼ ▼ ▼ ▼ ▼ ▼ ▼ ▼ ▼ ▼

USDA #267730

Botanical name: *Capsicum annuum* cv. 'Black Cuban'

Common name: piquin

Location: Cuba

Seed source: USDA

Pod length: .5 in.

Pod width: .5 in.

Immature color: black

Mature color: red

Comments: Nice ornamental plant. There is no black color in this pepper, just a very dark purple. Very pungent.

▼ ▼ ▼ ▼ ▼ ▼ ▼ ▼ ▼ ▼ ▼

USDA # none

Botanical name: *Capsicum annuum* cv. 'Black Prince'

Common name: ornamental

Location: USA

Seed source: Seed Savers Exchange

Pod length: .75 in.

Pod width: .5 in.

Immature color: black

Mature color: red

Comments: A striking ornamental. Very pungent.

▼ ▼ ▼ ▼ ▼ ▼ ▼ ▼ ▼ ▼ ▼

USDA # none

Botanical name: *Capsicum annuum* cv. 'NuMex Centennial'

Common names: ornamental, 'Firecracker,' 'Amethyst'

Location: New Mexico State University

Seed source: Enchanted Seeds

Pod length: .75 in.

Pod width: .5 in.

Immature color: purple

Mature color: red

Comments: Flower color is purple. Very pungent.

▼ ▼ ▼ ▼ ▼ ▼ ▼ ▼ ▼ ▼ ▼

USDA # none

Botanical name: *Capsicum annuum* cv. 'Treasure Red'

Common name: ornamental

Location: USA

Seed source: Park Seed Co.

Pod length: 1.5 in.

Pod width: .5 in.

Immature color: white

Mature color: red

Comments: Unusual immature white pods. Very pungent.

▼ ▼ ▼ ▼ ▼ ▼ ▼ ▼ ▼ ▼

USDA # none

Botanical name: *Capsicum
annuum* cv. 'Arledge Hot'

Common name: Arledge hot

Location: Louisiana, USA

Seed source: Seeds of Change

Pod length: 2.5 in.

Pod width: 1.25 in.

Immature color: green

Mature color: red

Comments: Very pungent.

▼ ▼ ▼ ▼ ▼ ▼ ▼ ▼ ▼ ▼

USDA # none

Botanical name: *Capsicum
annuum* cv. 'Marbles'

Common name: ornamental

Location: Oregon State University

Seed source: Territorial
Seed Co.

Pod length: .5 in.

Pod width: .75 in.

Immature color: white

Mature color: red

Comments: These ornamental
pods do look like
marbles!

▼ ▼ ▼ ▼ ▼ ▼ ▼ ▼ ▼ ▼ ▼

USDA # none

Botanical name: *Capsicum annuum* cv. 'Holiday Cheer'

Common names: holiday cheer, ornamental

Location: USA

Seed source: Park Seed Co.

Pod length: 1 in.

Pod width: 1 in.

Immature color: yellow

Mature color: red

Comments: Vigorous producer.

▼ ▼ ▼ ▼ ▼ ▼ ▼ ▼ ▼ ▼

USDA # none

Botanical name: *Capsicum annuum* cv. 'Puppy Pepper'

Common name: puppy pepper

Location: Costa Rica

Seed source: on location. Try Seed Savers Exchange

Pod length: .75 in.

Pod width: .5 in.

Immature color: yellow

Mature color: red

Comments: Nonpungent pepper cultivated in home gardens.

▼ ▼ ▼ ▼ ▼ ▼ ▼ ▼ ▼ ▼ ▼

USDA # none

Botanical name: *Capsicum annuum* cv. 'NuMex Twilight'

Common names: piquín, ornamental

Location: New Mexico State University

Seed source: Enchanted Seeds

Pod length: .75 in.

Pod width: .5 in.

Immature colors: purple and yellow

Mature colors: orange and red

Comments: Ornamental, flowers white. Very pungent.

▼ ▼ ▼ ▼ ▼ ▼ ▼ ▼ ▼ ▼ ▼

USDA # none

Botanical name: *Capsicum annuum* cv. 'NuMex Twilight'

Common names: piquín, ornamental

Location: Mexico

Seed source: Seed Savers Exchange

Pod length: .75 in.

Pod width: .5 in.

Immature colors: purple, yellow

Mature colors: orange, red

Comments: Flowers white. Very pungent. Grows well in a pot.

▼ ▼ ▼ ▼ ▼ ▼ ▼ ▼ ▼ ▼ ▼

USDA # none

Botanical name: *Capsicum annuum* cv. 'Poinsettia'

Common name: Japanese hot

Location: Japan

Seed source: The Pepper Gal

Pod length: 2 in.

Pod width: .25 in.

Immature color: green

Mature color: red

Comments: Similar to santaka; a nice ornamental. Very pungent.

▼ ▼ ▼ ▼ ▼ ▼ ▼ ▼ ▼ ▼ ▼

USDA # none

Botanical name: *Capsicum annuum* cv. 'Sweet Pickle'

Common names: sweet pickle, ornamental

Location: USA

Seed source: Park Seed

Pod length: 2 in.

Pod width: 1 in.

Immature color: yellow

Mature color: red

Comments: Striking ornamental. Nonpungent.

▼ ▼ ▼ ▼ ▼ ▼ ▼ ▼ ▼ ▼

USDA # none

Botanical name: *Capsicum annuum* cv. 'Fiesta'

Common names: fiesta, ornamental

Location: USA

Seed source: Park Seed

Pod length: 2 in.

Pod width: .25 in.

Immature color: yellow-orange

Mature color: red

Comments: Ornamental; many pods on small plants.

▼ ▼ ▼ ▼ ▼ ▼ ▼ ▼ ▼ ▼

USDA # none

Botanical name: *Capsicum annuum* cv. 'Bouquet'

Common name: ornamental

Location: USA

Seed source: The Pepper Gal

Pod length: .75 in.

Pod width: .5 in.

Immature color: green

Mature color: red

Comments: Flower color is purple.

▼ ▼ ▼ ▼ ▼ ▼ ▼ ▼ ▼ ▼ ▼

USDA # none

Botanical name: *Capsicum annuum* cv. 'Purira'

Common name: purira chile

Location: USA

Seed source: Seeds of Change

Pod length: 1.75 in.

Pod width: 1.5 in.

Immature color: purple-yellow

Mature color: red

Comments: Very pungent.

▼ ▼ ▼ ▼ ▼ ▼ ▼ ▼ ▼ ▼ ▼

USDA # none

Botanical name: *Capsicum annuum* cv. 'Large Cherry'

Common name: cherry pepper

Location: USA

Seed source: Nichols Garden Nursery

Pod length: 1 in.

Pod width: 1.5 in.

Immature color: green

Mature color: red

Comments: Good for pickling; mild heat.

▼ ▼ ▼ ▼ ▼ ▼ ▼ ▼ ▼ ▼ ▼

USDA # none

Botanical name: *Capsicum annuum* cv. 'Peter Pepper'

Common names: peter pepper; ornamental

Location: USA

Seed source: Enchanted Seeds

Pod length: 2.5 in.

Pod width: .25 in.

Immature color: green

Mature color: red

Comments: The meaning of the common name of this popular ornamental is fairly obvious. Mild pungency.

▼ ▼ ▼ ▼ ▼ ▼ ▼ ▼ ▼ ▼ ▼

USDA # none

Botanical name: *Capsicum annuum* cv. 'Coban'

Common name: chile cobán

Location: Guatemala

Seed source: Native Seeds/SEARCH

Pod length: .75 in.

Pod width: .5 in.

Immature color: green

Mature color: red

Comments: Piquín type; traditionally smoke-cured over wood fires. Very pungent.

▼ ▼ ▼ ▼ ▼ ▼ ▼ ▼ ▼ ▼ ▼

USDA # none

Botanical name: *Capsicum annuum* cv. 'Cabai Burong'

Common name: cabai burong

Location: Malaysia

Seed source: Redwood City Seed Co.

Pod length: 2 in.

Pod width: .5 in.

Immature color: green

Mature color: orange-red

Comments: *Cabai* means pepper.

▼ ▼ ▼ ▼ ▼ ▼ ▼ ▼ ▼ ▼ ▼

USDA # none

Botanical name: *Capsicum annuum* cv. 'Giant Thai Hot'

Common name: Asian hot

Location: R.E. Bernstrom, Kentucky

Seed source: Park Seed

Pod length: 1.25 in.

Pod width: .5 in.

Immature color: green

Mature color: red

Comments: Very pungent.

▼ ▼ ▼ ▼ ▼ ▼ ▼ ▼ ▼ ▼ ▼

USDA # none

Botanical name: *Capsicum annuum* cv. 'Chi-chien'

Common names: chi-chien, Asian hot

Location: China

Seed source: Evergreen Y.H. Enterprises

Pod length: 2.5 in.

Pod width: .5 in.

Immature color: light green

Mature color: red

Comments: Erect fruits, may be used as an ornamental. Very pungent.

▼ ▼ ▼ ▼ ▼ ▼ ▼ ▼ ▼ ▼ ▼

USDA # none

Botanical name: *Capsicum annuum* cv. 'Yatsafusa'

Common names: yatsafusa, Asian hot

Location: Japan

Seed source: Nichols Garden Nursery

Pod length: 2.5 in.

Pod width: .25 in.

Immature color: light green

Mature color: red

Comments: Very pungent; in Spanish called *chiles japones*.

▼ ▼ ▼ ▼ ▼ ▼ ▼ ▼ ▼ ▼ ▼

USDA # none

Botanical name: *Capsicum annuum* cv. 'Takanot-sume'

Common names: takanot-sume; Asian hot

Location: Japan

Seed source: Seed Savers Exchange

Pod length: 1.5 in.

Pod width: .5 in.

Immature color: green

Mature color: red

Comments: name means "claw of the eagle."

▼ ▼ ▼ ▼ ▼ ▼ ▼ ▼ ▼ ▼ ▼

USDA # none

Botanical name: *Capsicum annuum* cv. 'Kahari'

Common name: kahari

Location: Asia

Seed source: The Pepper Gal

Pod length: 1.75 in.

Pod width: .5 in.

Immature color: light green

Mature color: red

Comments: Similar to 'Yatsa-fusa,' page 115.

▼ ▼ ▼ ▼ ▼ ▼ ▼ ▼ ▼ ▼

USDA # none

Botanical name: *Capsicum annuum* cv. 'White Hot'

Common name: white hot

Location: USA

Seed source: The Pepper Gal

Pod length: 1.25 in.

Pod width: .25 in.

Immature color: white

Mature color: red

Comments: Striking ornamental.

▼ ▼ ▼ ▼ ▼ ▼ ▼ ▼ ▼ ▼

USDA # none

Botanical name: *Capsicum annuum* cv. 'Mississippi Sport'

Common name: Mississippi sport

Location: Mississippi

Seed source: Burgess

Pod length: 2 in.

Pod width: .5 in.

Immature color: green

Mature color: red

Comments: Pickled and served with Chicago hot dogs.

▼ ▼ ▼ ▼ ▼ ▼ ▼ ▼ ▼ ▼ ▼

USDA # none

Botanical name: *Capsicum annuum*

Common name: Cambodian flame tongue

Location: Cambodia

Seed source: collected on location; try Seed Savers Exchange

Pod length: 1.5 in.

Pod width: .25 in.

Immature color: green

Mature color: red

Comments: Collected and named by Richard Sterling. Very pungent.

▼ ▼ ▼ ▼ ▼ ▼ ▼ ▼ ▼ ▼ ▼

USDA #164185

Botanical name: *Capsicum annuum* cv. 'Mirch'

Common names: mirch, Asian hot

Location: India

Seed source: USDA

Pod length: 2 in.

Pod width: .5 in.

Immature color: green

Mature color: red

Comments: India is one of the largest pepper-producing countries. Very pungent.

▼ ▼ ▼ ▼ ▼ ▼ ▼ ▼ ▼ ▼

USDA # none

Botanical name: *Capsicum annuum*

Common name: yellow Thai

Location: Thailand

Seed source: Old Southwest Trading Company

Pod length: 3 in.

Pod width: .5 in.

Immature color: green

Mature color: yellow

Comments: Very attractive plant with bright yellow pods. Medium pungency.

▼ ▼ ▼ ▼ ▼ ▼ ▼ ▼ ▼ ▼

USDA #163186

Botanical name: *Capsicum annuum*

Common name: Asian hot

Location: India

Seed source: USDA

Pod length: 1.25 in.

Pod width: .5 in.

Immature color: green

Mature color: orange

Comments: Very pungent.

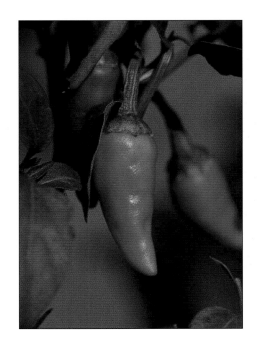

▼ ▼ ▼ ▼ ▼ ▼ ▼ ▼ ▼ ▼ ▼

USDA #439378

Botanical name: *Capsicum annuum* cv. 'Kitchen Pepper'

Common names: kitchen pepper, country pepper

Location: Jamaica

Seed source: USDA

Pod length: 1 in.

Pod width: .25 in.

Immature color: green

Mature color: red

Comments: Often grown outside kitchen windows in Jamaica. We saw one plant at the Good Hope Great House that was fifteen feet tall.

▼ ▼ ▼ ▼ ▼ ▼ ▼ ▼ ▼ ▼ ▼

USDA # none

Botanical name: *Capsicum annuum* cv. 'Hawaiian Sweet Hot'

Common name: Hawaiian sweet hot

Location: Hawaii

Seed source: Redwood Seed Co.

Pod length: 1.5 in.

Pod width: .5 in.

Immature color: green

Mature color: red

Comments: Pungent; the name is a contradiction in terms.

▼ ▼ ▼ ▼ ▼ ▼ ▼ ▼ ▼ ▼

USDA #574545

Botanical name: *Capsicum annuum* cv. 'Chile Blanco'

Common name: chile blanco

Location: Mexico

Seed source: USDA

Pod length: 1.5 in.

Pod width: .5 in.

Immature color: yellow

Mature color: red

Comments: White flower; should be called *chile amarillo*.

▼ ▼ ▼ ▼ ▼ ▼ ▼ ▼ ▼ ▼

USDA # none

Botanical name: *Capsicum annuum* cv. 'Hahony Kocho'

Common names: hahony kocho, Asian hot

Location: Korea

Seed source: The Pepper Gal

Pod length: 1.75 in.

Pod width: .25 in.

Immature color: green

Mature color: red

Comments: Used in *kimchi*, fermented cabbage with peppers.

▼ ▼ ▼ ▼ ▼ ▼ ▼ ▼ ▼ ▼ ▼

USDA # none

Botanical name: *Capsicum annuum* cv. 'Czechoslovakian Black'

Common name: Czechoslovakian black

Location: Czech Republic

Seed source: Seeds of Change

Pod length: 1.75 in.

Pod width: 1 in.

Immature color: black

Mature color: red

Comments: Flower color is purple.

▼ ▼ ▼ ▼ ▼ ▼ ▼ ▼ ▼ ▼ ▼

USDA # none

Botanical name: *Capsicum annuum* cv. 'Floral Gem'

Common name: floral gem

Location: USA

Seed source: The Pepper Gal

Pod length: 1.25 in.

Pod width: .75 in.

Immature color: yellow

Mature color: red

Comments: A wax pod type. Mild pungency.

▼ ▼ ▼ ▼ ▼ ▼ ▼ ▼ ▼ ▼

USDA # none

Botanical name: *Capsicum annuum* cv. 'Petite Sirah'

Common name: petite sirah

Location: USA

Seed source: Shepherd's Garden Seeds

Pod length: 2.5 in.

Pod width: 1 in.

Immature color: yellow

Mature color: red

Comments: A wax pod type. Medium pungency.

▼ ▼ ▼ ▼ ▼ ▼ ▼ ▼ ▼ ▼

USDA # none

Botanical name: *Capsicum annuum* cv. 'Xcatic'

Common names: chile xcatic, chile güero

Location: Yucatán Peninsula, Mexico

Seed source: collected on location by Nancy Gerlach; try Seed Savers Exchange

Pod length: 4.5 in.

Pod width: .75 in.

Immature color: yellow

Mature color: red

Comments: Wax pod type; this is a mild chile used in salsas.

▼ ▼ ▼ ▼ ▼ ▼ ▼ ▼ ▼ ▼ ▼

USDA # none

Botanical name: *Capsicum annuum* cv. 'Sweet Banana'

Common names: sweet banana, banana pepper

Location: USA

Seed source: Park Seeds

Pod length: 4 in.

Pod width: 1.25 in.

Immature color: yellow

Mature color: red

Comments: Wax pod type; a frying pepper. Mild.

▼ ▼ ▼ ▼ ▼ ▼ ▼ ▼ ▼ ▼ ▼

USDA # none

Botanical name: *Capsicum annuum* cv. 'Ivory Banana'

Common name: banana pepper

Location: USA

Seed source: Stokes

Pod length: 5.5 in.

Pod width: 1.75 in.

Immature color: ivory white

Mature color: red

Comments: Wax pod type; a frying pepper. Mild.

▼ ▼ ▼ ▼ ▼ ▼ ▼ ▼ ▼ ▼ ▼

USDA # none

Botanical name: *Capsicum annuum* cv. 'Hungarian Yellow Wax Hot'

Common name: yellow wax hot

Location: USA

Seed source: Seeds of Change

Pod length: 4 in.

Pod width: 1.5 in.

Immature color: yellow

Mature color: red

Comments: Wax pod type; mild pepper for frying or salads. Erect or pendant pods.

▼ ▼ ▼ ▼ ▼ ▼ ▼ ▼ ▼ ▼ ▼

USDA # none

Botanical name: *Capsicum annuum* cv. 'Cascabella'

Common name: cascabella

Location: USA

Seed source: Seed Savers Exchange

Pod length: 2 in.

Pod width: 1 in.

Immature color: yellow

Mature color: orange

Comments: Wax pod type; erect pods. Not to be confused with the Mexican *cascabel*. Mild.

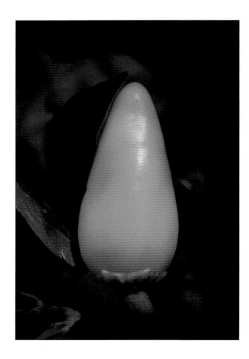

▼ ▼ ▼ ▼ ▼ ▼ ▼ ▼ ▼ ▼ ▼

USDA # none

Botanical name: *Capsicum annuum* cv. 'Santa Fe Grande'

Common name: Santa Fe grande

Location: USA

Seed source: Plants of the Southwest

Pod length: 2 in.

Pod width: 1 in.

Immature color: yellow

Mature color: orange

Comments: Developed by Dr. Paul Smith at the University of California at Davis. Wax pod type, mild.

▼ ▼ ▼ ▼ ▼ ▼ ▼ ▼ ▼ ▼ ▼

USDA # none

Botanical name: *Capsicum annuum* cv. 'Almapaprika'

Common name: Hungarian paprika

Location: Hungary

Seed source: VCRI

Pod length: 2.5 in.

Pod width: 2.5 in.

Immature color: white

Mature color: red

Comments: Paprika pods vary widely in terms of shape. Nonpungent.

▼ ▼ ▼ ▼ ▼ ▼ ▼ ▼ ▼ ▼ ▼

USDA #368409

Botanical name: *Capsicum annuum* cv. 'Ceresoviden'

Common name: paprika

Location: Yugoslavia

Seed source: USDA

Pod length: .75 in.

Pod width: .75 in.

Immature color: green

Mature color: red

Comments: Nonpungent.

▼ ▼ ▼ ▼ ▼ ▼ ▼ ▼ ▼ ▼ ▼

USDA # none

Botanical name: *Capsicum annuum* cv. 'Kujawianka'

Common name: paprika

Location: Poland

Seed source: VCRI

Pod length: 1.25 in.

Pod width: 3 in.

Immature color: white

Mature color: red

Comments: Nonpungent.

▼ ▼ ▼ ▼ ▼ ▼ ▼ ▼ ▼ ▼ ▼

USDA # none

Botanical name: *Capsicum annuum* cv. 'G. W. Cheese'

Common name: Hungarian paprika

Location: Hungary

Seed source: Stokes

Pod length: 1.25 in.

Pod width: 3 in.

Immature color: white

Mature color: red

Comments: Nonpungent.

▼ ▼ ▼ ▼ ▼ ▼ ▼ ▼ ▼ ▼ ▼

USDA # none

Botanical name: *Capsicum annuum* cv. 'Piknik'

Common name: Hungarian paprika

Location: Hungary

Seed source: VCRI

Pod length: 1.25 in.

Pod width: 3 in.

Immature color: green

Mature color: red

Comments: Nonpungent.

▼ ▼ ▼ ▼ ▼ ▼ ▼ ▼ ▼ ▼ ▼

USDA # none

Botanical name: *Capsicum annuum* cv. 'Paradison Alaku Zold Szentes'

Common name: Hungarian paprika

Location: Hungary

Seed source: Redwood City Seed Co.

Pod length: 1.25 in.

Pod width: 3 in.

Immature color: green

Mature color: red

Comments: Nonpungent.

▼ ▼ ▼ ▼ ▼ ▼ ▼ ▼ ▼ ▼ ▼

USDA # none

Botanical name: *Capsicum annuum* cv. 'Greyco'

Common name: Hungarian paprika

Location: Hungary

Seed source: Budadeteny Seeds

Pod length: 1.25 in.

Pod width: 3 in.

Immature color: green

Mature color: red

Comments: A very old pod type in Hungary; nonpungent.

▼ ▼ ▼ ▼ ▼ ▼ ▼ ▼ ▼ ▼

USDA # none

Botanical name: *Capsicum annuum* cv. 'Feberozon'

Common name: Hungarian paprika

Location: Hungary

Seed source: VCRI

Pod length: 4 in.

Pod width: 2.5 in.

Immature color: white

Mature color: red

Comments: Name means "waterfall." One of the most popular sweet peppers in Hungary.

▼ ▼ ▼ ▼ ▼ ▼ ▼ ▼ ▼ ▼

USDA # none

Botanical name: *Capsicum annuum* cv. 'D. Cecei'

Common name: Hungarian paprika

Location: Hungary

Seed source: Budateteny Seeds

Pod length: 3 in.

Pod width: 2.5 in.

Immature color: white

Mature color: red

Comments: Nonpungent, yellow wax type. Resistant to the tobacco etch virus.

▼ ▼ ▼ ▼ ▼ ▼ ▼ ▼ ▼ ▼ ▼

USDA # none

Botanical name: *Capsicum annuum* cv. 'Sobor'

Common name: Hungarian paprika

Location: Hungary

Seed source: Budateteny Seeds

Pod length: 5 in.

Pod width: 2.5 in.

Immature color: light green

Mature color: red

Comments: Mildly pungent.

▼ ▼ ▼ ▼ ▼ ▼ ▼ ▼ ▼ ▼ ▼

USDA # none

Botanical name: *Capsicum annuum* cv. 'Antohi Romanian'

Common name: paprika

Location: Romania

Seed source: Johnny's Selected Seeds

Pod length: 3.5 in.

Pod width: 2 in.

Immature color: white

Mature color: red

Comments: Named after a Romanian acrobat, Jan Antohi, who defected to the U.S. and brought seeds with him.

▼ ▼ ▼ ▼ ▼ ▼ ▼ ▼ ▼ ▼ ▼

USDA #555647

Botanical name: *Capsicum annuum* cv. 'Podarok Moldavi'

Common name: paprika

Location: Russia

Seed source: USDA

Pod length: 3.5 in.

Pod width: 1.75 in.

Immature color: yellow

Mature color: red

Comments: Reported to be resistant to verticillium wilt disease.

▼ ▼ ▼ ▼ ▼ ▼ ▼ ▼ ▼ ▼ ▼

USDA # none

Botanical name: *Capsicum annuum* cv. 'Roumanian Hot'

Common name: paprika

Location: Romania

Seed source: The Pepper Gal

Pod length: 3.25 in.

Pod width: 2.5 in.

Immature color: ivory

Mature color: red

Comments: Medium pungency.

▼ ▼ ▼ ▼ ▼ ▼ ▼ ▼ ▼ ▼ ▼

USDA # none

Botanical name: *Capsicum annuum* cv. 'Szentesi'

Common name: Hungarian paprika

Location: Hungary

Seed source: VCRI

Pod length: 4.25 in.

Pod width: 2 in.

Immature color: ivory

Mature color: red

Comments: Used as a spice; pungent.

▼ ▼ ▼ ▼ ▼ ▼ ▼ ▼ ▼ ▼

USDA # none

Botanical name: *Capsicum annuum* cv. 'Rubinova'

Common name: paprika

Location: Slovakia

Seed source: VCRI

Pod length: 3.5 in.

Pod width: 2 in.

Immature color: green

Mature color: red

Comments: Nonpungent.

▼ ▼ ▼ ▼ ▼ ▼ ▼ ▼ ▼ ▼ ▼

USDA # none

Botanical name: *Capsicum annuum* cv. 'Belecskay Zöld'

Common name: Hungarian paprika

Location: Hungary

Seed source: VCRI

Pod length: 3.25 in.

Pod width: 2.5 in.

Immature color: white

Mature color: red

Comments: Nonpungent.

▼ ▼ ▼ ▼ ▼ ▼ ▼ ▼ ▼ ▼ ▼

USDA #357434

Botanical name: *Capsicum annuum* cv. 'Bela Babura'

Common name: paprika

Location: Yugoslavia

Seed source: USDA

Pod length: 4 in.

Pod width: 1.5 in.

Immature color: yellow

Mature color: red

Comments: Nonpungent.

▼ ▼ ▼ ▼ ▼ ▼ ▼ ▼ ▼ ▼

USDA # none

Botanical name: *Capsicum annuum* cv. 'Cyklon'

Common name: paprika

Location: Poland

Seed source: VCRI

Pod length: 5 in.

Pod width: 2.5 in.

Immature color: green

Mature color: red

Comments: Nonpungent.

▼ ▼ ▼ ▼ ▼ ▼ ▼ ▼ ▼ ▼

USDA # none

Botanical name: *Capsicum annuum* cv. 'Rekord'

Common name: Hungarian paprika

Location: Hungary

Seed source: VCRI

Pod length: 3.5 in.

Pod width: 2.5 in.

Immature color: green

Mature color: red

Comments: Nonpungent.

▼ ▼ ▼ ▼ ▼ ▼ ▼ ▼ ▼ ▼ ▼

USDA # none

Botanical name: *Capsicum annuum* cv. 'Kalocsai Det.'

Common name: Hungarian paprika

Location: Hungary

Seed source: VCRI

Pod length: 5 in.

Pod width: 1 in.

Immature color: green

Mature color: red

Comments: Named after the famous Hungarian paprika city, Kalocs.

▼ ▼ ▼ ▼ ▼ ▼ ▼ ▼ ▼ ▼ ▼

USDA # none

Botanical name: *Capsicum annuum* cv. 'Viktoria'

Common name: Hungarian paprika

Location: Hungary

Seed source: VCRI

Pod length: 5 in.

Pod width: 2 in.

Immature color: green

Mature color: red

Comments: Nonpungent.

▼ ▼ ▼ ▼ ▼ ▼ ▼ ▼ ▼ ▼ ▼

USDA # none

Botanical name: *Capsicum annuum* cv. 'Corbaci'

Common name: Hungarian paprika

Location: Hungary

Seed source: Redwood City Seed Co.

Pod length: 6.75 in.

Pod width: .75 in.

Immature color: light green

Mature color: red

Comments: Nonpungent

▼ ▼ ▼ ▼ ▼ ▼ ▼ ▼ ▼ ▼ ▼

USDA # none

Botanical name: *Capsicum annuum* cv. 'Calistan'

Common name: calistan

Location: Turkey

Seed source: Redwood City Seed Co.

Pod length: 6.25 in.

Pod width: 1.5 in.

Immature color: yellow

Mature color: red

Comments: Nonpungent.

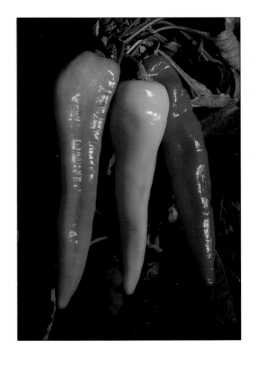

▼ ▼ ▼ ▼ ▼ ▼ ▼ ▼ ▼ ▼

USDA # none

Botanical name: *Capsicum annuum* cv. 'Malahat'

Common name: malahat

Location: Turkey

Seed source: The Pepper Gal

Pod length: 4 in.

Pod width: .75 in.

Immature color: green

Mature color: red

Comments: Very pungent.

▼ ▼ ▼ ▼ ▼ ▼ ▼ ▼ ▼ ▼

USDA # none

Botanical name: *Capsicum annuum* cv. 'Short Afghan'

Common name: Asian hot

Location: Afghanistan

Seed source: The Pepper Gal

Pod length: 2.25 in.

Pod width: .25 in.

Immature color: green

Mature color: red

Comments: Very pungent.

▼ ▼ ▼ ▼ ▼ ▼ ▼ ▼ ▼ ▼

USDA #294453

Botanical name: *Capsicum annuum* cv. 'Elsita'

Common name: elsita

Location: Virgin Islands

Seed source: USDA

Pod length: 1.25 in.

Pod width: 1 in.

Immature color: green

Mature color: red

Comments: Medium pungency.

▼ ▼ ▼ ▼ ▼ ▼ ▼ ▼ ▼ ▼

USDA #194908

Botanical name: *Capsicum annuum* cv. 'Ethiopian Hot'

Common name: Ethiopian hot

Location: Ethiopia

Seed source: USDA

Pod length: 2 in.

Pod width: 1 in.

Immature color: green

Mature color: red

Comments: Very pungent.

▼ ▼ ▼ ▼ ▼ ▼ ▼ ▼ ▼ ▼ ▼

USDA # none

Botanical name: *Capsicum annuum* cv. 'PC-1'

Common name: Asian hot

Location: India

Seed source: Redwood City Seed Co.

Pod length: 3 in.

Pod width: .5 in.

Immature color: green

Mature color: red

Comments: Very pungent.

▼ ▼ ▼ ▼ ▼ ▼ ▼ ▼ ▼ ▼ ▼

USDA # none

Botanical name: *Capsicum annuum* cv. 'Fresno'

Common name: Fresno

Location: U.S.A.

Seed source: Seeds of Change

Pod length: 2.5 in.

Pod width: 1 in.

Immature color: green

Mature color: red

Comments: New Mexican type; erect fruits, medium pungency.

▼ ▼ ▼ ▼ ▼ ▼ ▼ ▼ ▼ ▼ ▼

USDA # none

Botanical name: *Capsicum annuum*. cv. 'NuMex Sunflare'

Common name: sunflare

Location: New Mexico State University

Seed source: Enchanted Seeds

Pod length: 3 in.

Pod width: .75 in.

Immature color: green

Mature color: red

Comments: Erect fruits; can be used as ornamental. Very pungent.

▼ ▼ ▼ ▼ ▼ ▼ ▼ ▼ ▼ ▼ ▼

USDA # none

Botanical name: *Capsicum annuum* cv. 'NuMex Sunburst'

Common name: sunburst

Location: New Mexico State University

Seed source: Enchanted Seeds

Pod length: 3.2 in.

Pod width: .6 in.

Immature color: green

Mature color: orange

Comments: Used to make orange ristras. Very pungent.

▼ ▼ ▼ ▼ ▼ ▼ ▼ ▼ ▼ ▼ ▼

USDA # none

Botanical name: *Capsicum annuum* cv. 'NuMex Sunglo'

Common name: sunglo

Location: New Mexico State University

Seed source: Enchanted Seeds

Pod length: 3 in.

Pod width: .5 in.

Immature color: green

Mature color: yellow

Comments: Used to make yellow ristras. Very pungent.

▼ ▼ ▼ ▼ ▼ ▼ ▼ ▼ ▼ ▼

USDA # none

Botanical name: *Capsicum annuum* cv. 'Cochiti'

Common name: Cochiti chile

Location: USA

Seed source: Native Seeds/SEARCH

Pod length: 1.5 in.

Pod width: 1 in.

Immature color: green

Mature color: red

Comments: Grown on Cochiti Pueblo, New Mexico; medium pungency.

▼ ▼ ▼ ▼ ▼ ▼ ▼ ▼ ▼ ▼ ▼

USDA #209589

Botanical name: *Capsicum annuum* cv. 'Sazonadores Eachuch'

Common name: sazonador

Location: Cuba

Seed source: USDA

Pod length: 1.75 in.

Pod width: .75 in.

Immature color: green

Mature color: red

Comments: Originally described as a "tabasco type," but not a *C. frutescens* as fruit is too large for that species. Medium pungency.

▼ ▼ ▼ ▼ ▼ ▼ ▼ ▼ ▼ ▼

USDA #439431

Botanical name: *Capsicum annuum* cv. 'Fiji Hot'

Common name: Fiji hot

Location: Fiji

Seed source: USDA

Pod length: 2.75 in.

Pod width: .5 in.

Immature color: green

Mature color: red

Comments: Very pungent.

▼ ▼ ▼ ▼ ▼ ▼ ▼ ▼ ▼ ▼ ▼

USDA #495790

Botanical name: *Capsicum annuum* cv. 'Plovdivska Sipka'

Common name: unknown

Location: Bulgaria

Seed source: USDA

Pod length: 2 in.

Pod width: .75 in.

Immature color: green

Mature color: red

Comments: Very pungent.

▼ ▼ ▼ ▼ ▼ ▼ ▼ ▼ ▼ ▼

USDA #187315

Botanical name: *Capsicum annuum* cv. 'Pimenta Mexicana'

Common names: pimenta Mexicana, Mexican pepper

Location: Guatemala

Seed source: USDA

Pod length: 1.5 in.

Pod width: .5 in.

Immature color: green

Mature color: red

Comments: Nonpungent.

▼ ▼ ▼ ▼ ▼ ▼ ▼ ▼ ▼ ▼ ▼

USDA # none

Botanical name: *Capsicum annuum* cv. 'Mirasol'

Common name: mirasol

Location: Mexico

Seed source: Enchanted Seeds

Pod length: 4.25 in.

Pod width: .75 in.

Immature color: green

Mature color: red

Comments: Some fruits are erect; even though these are pendant, they are still mirasols because of their translucent fruit and fruity flavor. Medium pungency.

▼ ▼ ▼ ▼ ▼ ▼ ▼ ▼ ▼ ▼ ▼

USDA # none

Botanical name: *Capsicum annuum* cv. 'NuMex Mirasol'

Common name: NuMex mirasol

Location: New Mexico State University

Seed source: Enchanted Seeds

Pod length: 2.25 in.

Pod width: .75 in.

Immature color: green

Mature color: red

Comments: Developed at NMSU for increased yield. Medium pungency.

▼ ▼ ▼ ▼ ▼ ▼ ▼ ▼ ▼ ▼

USDA #281389

Botanical name: *Capsicum annuum* cv. 'Guajillo'

Common name: guajillo

Location: Mexico

Seed source: USDA

Pod length: 3.25 in.

Pod width: .75 in.

Immature color: green

Mature color: burgundy

Comments: A very popular dry chile in Mexico; may be progenitor to the New Mexican pod type. Medium pungency.

▼ ▼ ▼ ▼ ▼ ▼ ▼ ▼ ▼ ▼

USDA # none

Botanical name: *Capsicum annuum* cv. 'Chile de Comida'

Common name: guajillo

Location: Mexico

Seed source: J.L. Hudson, Seedsman

Pod length: 4 in.

Pod width: 1 in.

Immature color: green

Mature color: red

Comments: The name, chile of food, is an allusion to its culinary popularity. Grown primarily in Zacatecas, Durango, and Aguascalientes. Medium pungency.

▼ ▼ ▼ ▼ ▼ ▼ ▼ ▼ ▼ ▼

USDA # none

Botanical name: *Capsicum annuum* cv. 'Chile In-ayague'

Common name: chile in-ayague

Location: Mexico

Seed source: J.L. Hudson, Seedsman

Pod length: 1.5 in.

Pod width: .75 in.

Immature color: green

Mature color: red

Comments: Very pungent.

▼ ▼ ▼ ▼ ▼ ▼ ▼ ▼ ▼ ▼

USDA # none

Botanical name: *Capsicum annuum* cv. 'Pulla'

Common names: pulla, puya

Location: Mexico

Seed source: Enchanted Seeds

Pod length: 3.5 in.

Pod width: .75 in.

Immature color: green

Mature color: red

Comments: A debate rages whether this is a form of de árbol, guajillo, or mirasol. Medium pungency.

▼ ▼ ▼ ▼ ▼ ▼ ▼ ▼ ▼ ▼ ▼

USDA # none

Botanical name: *Capsicum annuum* cv. 'de árbol'

Common name: chile de árbol

Location: Mexico

Seed sources: Mojave Spice Co., Native Seeds/SEARCH

Pod length: 2.5 in.

Pod width: .25 in.

Immature color: green

Mature color: red

Comments: Name means "treelike chile," an allusion to its habit. Grown primarily in Jalisco and Nayarit. Medium pungency.

▼ ▼ ▼ ▼ ▼ ▼ ▼ ▼ ▼ ▼ ▼

USDA # none

Botanical name: *Capsicum annuum* cv. 'Hot Portugal'

Common name: hot Portugal

Location: Portugal

Seed source: Stokes Seed

Pod length: 4.5 in.

Pod width: .75 in.

Immature color: green

Mature color: red

Comments: Very pungent.

▼ ▼ ▼ ▼ ▼ ▼ ▼ ▼ ▼ ▼ ▼

USDA # none

Botanical name: *Capsicum annuum* cv. 'Demre'

Common names: demre, Turkish hot

Location: Turkey

Seed source: Redwood City Seed Co.

Pod length: 5 in.

Pod width: .75 in.

Immature color: green

Mature color: red

Comments: Very cayennelike. Very pungent.

▼ ▼ ▼ ▼ ▼ ▼ ▼ ▼ ▼ ▼ ▼

USDA # none

Botanical name: *Capsicum annuum* cv. 'Dunso'

Common names: dunso, Turkish hot

Location: Turkey

Seed source: The Pepper Gal

Pod length: 2.25 in.

Pod width: .25 in.

Immature color: yellow-green

Mature color: red

Comments: Very pungent.

▼ ▼ ▼ ▼ ▼ ▼ ▼ ▼ ▼ ▼ ▼

USDA # none

Botanical name: *Capsicum annuum* cv. 'Desi Teekhi'

Common names: desi teekhi, Asian hot

Location: India

Seed source: The Pepper Gal

Pod length: 3.5 in.

Pod width: .5 in.

Immature color: green

Mature color: red

Comments: Very cayennelike. Very pungent.

▼ ▼ ▼ ▼ ▼ ▼ ▼ ▼ ▼ ▼

USDA # none

Botanical name: *Capsicum annuum* cv. 'Pusa Jwala'

Common names: pusa jwala, Asian hot

Location: Indonesia

Seed source: Seed Savers Exchange

Pod length: 4.5 in.

Pod width: .25 in.

Immature color: light green

Mature color: red

Comments: Very cayennelike. Very pungent.

▼ ▼ ▼ ▼ ▼ ▼ ▼ ▼ ▼ ▼

USDA #162606

Botanical name: *Capsicum annuum* cv. 'Niu Chiao Chiao'

Common names: niu chiao chiao, Asian hot

Location: China

Seed source:USDA

Pod length: 3.75 in.

Pod width: .75 in.

Immature color: green

Mature color: red

Comments: Very pungent. The name means "bull's horn."

▼ ▼ ▼ ▼ ▼ ▼ ▼ ▼ ▼ ▼

USDA # none

Botanical name: *Capsicum annuum* cv. 'Paper Dragon'

Common names: paper dragon, Asian hot

Location: China

Seed source: Johnny's Selected Seeds

Pod length: 4 in.

Pod width: .5 in.

Immature color: yellow-green

Mature color: red

Comments: Thin fleshed; medium pungency.

▼ ▼ ▼ ▼ ▼ ▼ ▼ ▼ ▼ ▼ ▼

USDA # none

Botanical name: *Capsicum annuum* cv. 'Pungent Pride'

Common names: pungent pride, Asian hot

Location: India

Seed source: Redwood City Seed Co.

Pod length: 4.25 in.

Pod width: .25 in.

Immature color: light green

Mature color: red

Comments: Sometimes mislabeled as *C. frutescens*. Very pungent.

▼ ▼ ▼ ▼ ▼ ▼ ▼ ▼ ▼ ▼ ▼

USDA # none

Botanical name: *Capsicum annuum* cv. 'Yung Go'

Common names: yung go, Asian hot

Location: China

Seed source: The Pepper Gal

Pod length: 5 in.

Pod width: .5 in.

Immature color: green

Mature color: red

Comments: Very cayennelike. Very pungent. The name means "sheep's horn."

▼ ▼ ▼ ▼ ▼ ▼ ▼ ▼ ▼ ▼ ▼

USDA # none

Botanical name: *Capsicum annuum* cv. 'Korean Hot'

Common name: Korean hot

Location: Korea

Seed source: Hungnong Seed Co.

Pod length: 5.25 in.

Pod width: .5 in.

Immature color: green

Mature color: red

Comments: Very pungent.

▼ ▼ ▼ ▼ ▼ ▼ ▼ ▼ ▼ ▼

USDA # none

Botanical name: *Capsicum annuum* cv. 'Dallas'

Common names: Dallas, Asian hot

Location: China

Seed source: The Pepper Gal

Pod length: 3.5 in.

Pod width: .75 in.

Immature color: green

Mature color: red

Comments: Often grown as an ornamental. Very pungent.

▼ ▼ ▼ ▼ ▼ ▼ ▼ ▼ ▼ ▼ ▼

USDA # none

Botanical name: *Capsicum annuum* cv. 'Merah'

Common names: merah, Asian hot

Location: Malaysia

Seed source: The Pepper Gal

Pod length: 4.75 in.

Pod width: 1 in.

Immature color: green

Mature color: red

Comments: Sometimes mislabeled as *C. frutescens*. Very pungent.

▼ ▼ ▼ ▼ ▼ ▼ ▼ ▼ ▼ ▼ ▼

USDA # none

Botanical name: *Capsicum annuum* cv. 'Sentinel'

Common names: sentinel, Turkish sweet

Location: Turkey

Seed source: Redwood City Seeds

Pod length: 5 in.

Pod width: .5 in.

Immature color: green

Mature color: red

Comments: Nonpungent but very cayennelike.

▼ ▼ ▼ ▼ ▼ ▼ ▼ ▼ ▼ ▼ ▼

USDA # none

Botanical name: *Capsicum annuum* cv. 'Aci Sivri'

Common names: aci sivri, Turkish hot

Location: Turkey

Seed source: Redwood City Seed Co.

Pod length: 5.5 in.

Pod width: .5 in.

Immature color: light green

Mature color: red

Comments: Very pungent.

▼ ▼ ▼ ▼ ▼ ▼ ▼ ▼ ▼ ▼ ▼

USDA #194722

Botanical name: *Capsicum annuum* cv. 'Pili Pili'

Common name: pili-pili

Location: Ethiopia

Seed source: USDA

Pod length: 3.25 in.

Pod width: .25 in.

Immature color: green

Mature color: red

Comments: The name means "pepper-pepper" in Swahili, and many African pod shapes are known by this term. Very pungent.

▼ ▼ ▼ ▼ ▼ ▼ ▼ ▼ ▼ ▼ ▼

USDA # none

Botanical name: *Capsicum annuum* cv. 'Large Thick Cayenne'

Common name: cayenne

Location: USA

Seed source: Enchanted Seeds

Pod length: 5.5 in.

Pod width: .75 in.

Immature color: green

Mature color: red

Comments: High pungency; pods begin erect, gradually become pendant.

▼ ▼ ▼ ▼ ▼ ▼ ▼ ▼ ▼ ▼ ▼

USDA # none

Botanical name: *Capsicum annuum* cv. 'Long Slim Cayenne'

Common name: cayenne

Location: USA

Seed source: Enchanted Seeds

Pod length: 3.25 in.

Pod width: .5 in.

Immature color: green

Mature color: red

Comments: Very pungent.

▼ ▼ ▼ ▼ ▼ ▼ ▼ ▼ ▼ ▼ ▼

USDA # none

Botanical name: *Capsicum annuum* cv. 'Ring of Fire'

Common name: cayenne

Location: USA

Seed source: Seeds of Change

Pod length: 3 in.

Pod width: .5 in.

Immature color: green

Mature color: red

Comments: Very pungent.

▼ ▼ ▼ ▼ ▼ ▼ ▼ ▼ ▼ ▼ ▼

USDA # none

Botanical name: *Capsicum annuum* cv. 'Carolina Cayenne'

Common name: cayenne

Location: USA

Seed source: The Pepper Gal

Pod length: 3 in.

Pod width: .75 in.

Immature color: green

Mature color: red

Comments: Very pungent. Excellent source of root-knot nematode resistance.

▼ ▼ ▼ ▼ ▼ ▼ ▼ ▼ ▼ ▼ ▼

USDA # none

Botanical name: *Capsicum annuum* cv. 'Charleston Hot'

Common name: cayenne

Location: USA

Seed source: The Pepper Gal

Pod length: 4 in.

Pod width: .5 in.

Immature color: green

Mature color: red

Comments: Very pungent.

▼ ▼ ▼ ▼ ▼ ▼ ▼ ▼ ▼ ▼ ▼

USDA # none

Botanical name: *Capsicum annuum* cv. 'Super Cayenne'

Common name: cayenne

Location: USA

Seed source: Nichols Garden Nursery

Pod length: 2 in.

Pod width: .5 in.

Immature color: green

Mature color: red

Comments: Very pungent.

▼ ▼ ▼ ▼ ▼ ▼ ▼ ▼ ▼ ▼ ▼

USDA # none

Botanical name: *Capsicum annuum* cv. 'Nardello'

Common name: Italian frying

Location: Italy

Seed source: Seeds of Change

Pod length: 4.75 in.

Pod width: .75 in.

Immature color: green

Mature color: red

Comments: Pepper is sliced and fried in olive oil. Nonpungent.

▼ ▼ ▼ ▼ ▼ ▼ ▼ ▼ ▼ ▼

USDA # none

Botanical name: *Capsicum annuum* cv. 'Italian Long'

Common name: Italian frying

Location: Italy

Seed source: Seed Savers Exchange

Pod length: 5 in.

Pod width: 2.25 in.

Immature color: green

Mature color: red

Comments: Pepper is sliced and fried in olive oil. Nonpungent.

▼ ▼ ▼ ▼ ▼ ▼ ▼ ▼ ▼ ▼ ▼

USDA # none

Botanical name: *Capsicum annuum* cv. 'Biscayne'

Common name: Cuban

Location: USA

Seed source: Nichols Garden Nursery

Pod length: 5.5 in.

Pod width: 2.5 in.

Immature color: light green

Mature color: red

Comments: Nonpungent. Large fruits, Cuban pod type.

▼ ▼ ▼ ▼ ▼ ▼ ▼ ▼ ▼ ▼ ▼

USDA # none

Botanical name: *Capsicum annuum* cv. 'Cubanelle'

Common name: Cuban

Location: Cuba

Seed source: Seed Savers Exchange

Pod length: 5.5 in.

Pod width: 2.5 in.

Immature colors: green, yellow

Mature colors: orange, red

Comments: A good pepper for frying in olive oil. Mildly pungent.

▼ ▼ ▼ ▼ ▼ ▼ ▼ ▼ ▼ ▼ ▼

USDA # none

Botanical name: *Capsicum annuum* cv. 'Pepper-oncini'

Common name: Italian frying

Location: Italy

Seed source: Shepherd's Garden Seeds

Pod length: 2.5 in.

Pod width: .75 in.

Immature color: green

Mature color: red

Comments: These peppers are also pickled. Mildly pungent.

▼ ▼ ▼ ▼ ▼ ▼ ▼ ▼ ▼ ▼ ▼

USDA # none

Botanical name: *Capsicum annuum* cv. 'Yellow Corno de Toro'

Common name: Italian frying

Location: Italy

Seed source: Shepherd's Garden Seeds

Pod length: 6 in.

Pod width: 1.5 in.

Immature color: green

Mature color: yellow

Comments: The name means bull horn. Nonpungent.

▼ ▼ ▼ ▼ ▼ ▼ ▼ ▼ ▼ ▼ ▼

USDA # none

Botanical name: *Capsicum annuum* cv. 'Red Corno de Toro'

Common name: Italian frying

Location: Italy

Seed source: Shepherd's Garden Seeds

Pod length: 6 in.

Pod width: 1.5 in.

Immature color: green

Mature color: red

Comments: Nonpungent.

▼ ▼ ▼ ▼ ▼ ▼ ▼ ▼ ▼ ▼ ▼

USDA # none

Botanical name: *Capsicum annuum* cv. 'Shishito'

Common name: Japanese sweet

Location: Japan

Seed source: Evergreen Y.H. Enterprises

Pod length: 2.5 in.

Pod width: .75 in.

Immature color: green

Mature color: red

Comments: Nonpungent, used in salads or pickled.

▼ ▼ ▼ ▼ ▼ ▼ ▼ ▼ ▼ ▼ ▼

USDA # none

Botanical name: *Capsicum annuum* cv. 'Japanese Fushimi'

Common name: Japanese sweet

Location: Japan

Seed source: Evergreen Y.H. Enterprises

Pod length: 5 in.

Pod width: .75 in.

Immature color: green

Mature color: red

Comments: Nonpungent.

▼ ▼ ▼ ▼ ▼ ▼ ▼ ▼ ▼ ▼ ▼

USDA # none

Botanical name: *Capsicum annuum* cv. 'Viejo Arruga Dulce'

Common name: viejo arruga dulce

Location: Mexico

Seed source: Redwood City Seed Co.

Pod length: 3 in.

Pod width: 1 in.

Immature color: green

Mature color: red

Comments: Name means "wrinkled sweet old man." Nonpungent.

▼ ▼ ▼ ▼ ▼ ▼ ▼ ▼ ▼ ▼

USDA # none

Botanical name: *Capsicum annuum* cv. 'Marconi Rosso'

Common name: Italian frying pepper

Location: Italy

Seed source: Burgess Plant & Seed Co.

Pod length: 6 in.

Pod width: 2.5 in.

Immature color: green

Mature color: red

Comments: Nonpungent.

▼ ▼ ▼ ▼ ▼ ▼ ▼ ▼ ▼ ▼

USDA # none

Botanical name: *Capsicum annuum* cv. 'Pimiento'

Common name: pimiento

Location: USA

Seed source: Enchanted Seeds

Pod length: 3 in.

Pod width: 2.25 in.

Immature color: green

Mature color: red

Comments: This is the familiar, nonpungent olive-stuffing pepper. It is sometimes dried, ground, and sold in the U.S. as paprika.

▼ ▼ ▼ ▼ ▼ ▼ ▼ ▼ ▼ ▼ ▼

USDA # none

Botanical name: *Capsicum annuum* cv. 'Sheepnose Pimiento'

Common name: pimiento

Location: USA

Seed source: Heritage Farm

Pod length: 1 in.

Pod width: 2.25 in.

Immature color: green

Mature color: red

Comments: Nonpungent.

▼ ▼ ▼ ▼ ▼ ▼ ▼ ▼ ▼ ▼ ▼

USDA # none

Botanical name: *Capsicum annuum* cv. 'Yellow Cheese Pimiento'

Common name: pimiento

Location: USA

Seed source: Stokes Seeds

Pod length: 1.5 in.

Pod width: 3 in.

Immature color: green

Mature color: orange

Comments: Striking nonpungent pods that resemble tomatoes.

▼ ▼ ▼ ▼ ▼ ▼ ▼ ▼ ▼ ▼ ▼

USDA # none

Botanical name: *Capsicum annuum* cv. 'Canada Cheese'

Common name: pimiento

Location: USA

Seed source: Stokes Seed

Pod length: 1.25 in.

Pod width: 2 in.

Immature color: green

Mature color: red

Comments: Nonpungent.

▼ ▼ ▼ ▼ ▼ ▼ ▼ ▼ ▼ ▼ ▼

USDA # none

Botanical name: *Capsicum annuum* cv. 'Spanish Paprika'

Common name: paprika

Location: Spain

Seed source: Seed Savers Exchange

Pod length: 1.5 in.

Pod width: 1.25 in.

Immature colors: ivory, green

Mature color: red

Comments: Nonpungent. Spain grows much of the world's paprika.

▼ ▼ ▼ ▼ ▼ ▼ ▼ ▼ ▼ ▼ ▼

USDA #298646

Botanical name: *Capsicum annuum* cv. 'Spanish Paprika'

Common name: Spanish paprika

Location: Spain

Seed source: USDA

Pod length: 1.25 in.

Pod width: 1.5 in.

Immature color: green

Mature color: red

Comments: Nonpungent.

▼ ▼ ▼ ▼ ▼ ▼ ▼ ▼ ▼ ▼ ▼

USDA # none

Botanical name: *Capsicum annuum* cv. 'Yellow Squash'

Common name: squash pepper

Location: USA

Seed source: The Pepper Gal

Pod length: 2 in.

Pod width: 1.25 in.

Immature color: yellow

Mature color: orange

Comments: Nonpungent.

▼ ▼ ▼ ▼ ▼ ▼ ▼ ▼ ▼ ▼ ▼

USDA # none

Botanical name: *Capsicum annuum* cv. 'Red Squash'

Common name: squash pepper

Location: USA

Seed source: The Pepper Gal

Pod length: 2 in.

Pod width: 1.25 in.

Immature color: green

Mature color: red

Comments: Nonpungent.

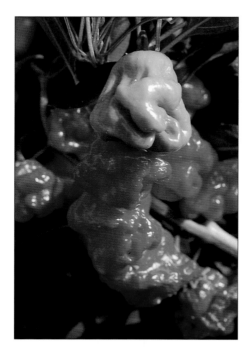

▼ ▼ ▼ ▼ ▼ ▼ ▼ ▼ ▼ ▼ ▼

USDA # none

Botanical name: *Capsicum annuum* cv. 'Mushroom'

Common name: mushroom pepper

Location: USA

Seed source: The Pepper Gal

Pod length: 1.5 in.

Pod width: 1.5 in.

Immature color: green

Mature color: red

Comments: Squash type, nonpungent.

▼ ▼ ▼ ▼ ▼ ▼ ▼ ▼ ▼ ▼ ▼

USDA # none

Botanical name: *Capsicum annuum* cv. 'Early Scotch Bonnet'

Common name: kitchen pepper

Location: Jamaica

Seed source: Stokes

Pod length: 1 in.

Pod width: 1.25 in.

Immature color: green

Mature color: red

Comments: The only Scotch bonnet that is *C. annuum*; the name is a misnomer. Mild pungency.

▼ ▼ ▼ ▼ ▼ ▼ ▼ ▼ ▼ ▼ ▼

USDA # none

Botanical name: *Capsicum annuum* cv. 'Cascabel'

Common names: chile cascabel, bola, bolita, and boludo

Location: Mexico

Seed source: Enchanted Seeds

Pod length: 1 in.

Pod width: 1 in.

Immature color: green

Mature color: red

Comments: When dry, the loose seeds cause the pod to rattle. Dried, cascabels are also known as coras and guajones. Grown in Jalisco and Guerrero. Medium pungency.

▼ ▼ ▼ ▼ ▼ ▼ ▼ ▼ ▼ ▼ ▼

USDA # none

Botanical name: *Capsicum annuum* cv. 'Chile de Agua'

Common name: chile de agua

Location: Mexico

Seed source: collected in Oaxaca Market; try Seed Savers Exchange

Pod length: 3 in.

Pod width: 1 in.

Immature color: green

Mature color: red

Comments: This interesting, erect-podded chile is used both green and dried red in Oaxaca. Medium pungency.

▼ ▼ ▼ ▼ ▼ ▼ ▼ ▼ ▼ ▼ ▼

USDA # none

Botanical name: *Capsicum annuum* cv. 'Costeño Amarillo'

Common name: costeño amarillo

Location: Mexico

Seed source: Seed Savers Exchange

Pod length: 2.5 in.

Pod width: .5 in.

Immature color: green

Mature color: yellowish orange

Comments: An Oaxacan chile used in mole sauces. Medium pungency.

▼ ▼ ▼ ▼ ▼ ▼ ▼ ▼ ▼ ▼ ▼

USDA # none

Botanical name: *Capsicum annuum* cv. 'Serrano Huasteco'

Common name: chile serrano

Location: Mexico

Seed source: Shepherd's Garden Seed

Pod length: 1.75 in.

Pod width: .5 in.

Immature color: green

Mature color: red

Comments: Grown all over Mexico, but primarily in Nayarit, San Luis Potosí, Sinaloa, and Tamaulipas. Medium pungency.

▼ ▼ ▼ ▼ ▼ ▼ ▼ ▼ ▼ ▼ ▼

USDA # none

Botanical name: *Capsicum annuum* cv. 'Sinahusia'

Common name: chile serrano

Location: Mexico

Seed source: Native Seeds/SEARCH

Pod length: 2 in.

Pod width: .5 in.

Immature color: green

Mature color: red

Comments: The word "serrano" means "from the highlands." Medium pungency.

▼ ▼ ▼ ▼ ▼ ▼ ▼ ▼ ▼ ▼ ▼

USDA # none

Botanical name: *Capsicum annuum* cv. 'Serrano Balin'

Common name: chile serrano

Location: Mexico

Seed source: Seed Savers Exchange

Pod length: 1.25 in.

Pod width: .5 in.

Immature color: green

Mature color: red

Comments: "Balin" means bullet. Serranos are used fresh in Mexico and also pickled commercially. Medium pungency.

▼ ▼ ▼ ▼ ▼ ▼ ▼ ▼ ▼ ▼ ▼

USDA # none

Botanical name: *Capsicum annuum* cv. 'Early Jalapeño'

Common name: jalapeño

Location: Mexico

Seed source: Enchanted Seeds

Pod length: 2.25 in.

Pod width: 1 in.

Immature color: green

Mature color: red

Comments: Jalapeños are one of the most popular Mexican peppers; they are used in salsas and are also pickled. Medium pungency.

▼ ▼ ▼ ▼ ▼ ▼ ▼ ▼ ▼ ▼ ▼

USDA # none

Botanical name: *Capsicum annuum* cv. 'Jumbo Jalapeño'

Common name: jalapeño

Location: Mexico

Seed source: Enchanted Seeds

Pod length: 2.25 in.

Pod width: 1.25 in.

Immature color: green

Mature color: red

Comments: Jalapeños are also called cuaresmeños in Mexico. Medium pungency.

▼ ▼ ▼ ▼ ▼ ▼ ▼ ▼ ▼ ▼ ▼

USDA # none

Botanical name: *Capsicum annuum* cv. 'Chilhuacle Amarillo'

Common name: yellow chilhuacle

Location: Mexico

Seed source: Seed Savers Exchange

Pod length: 3.25 in.

Pod width: 1.25 in.

Immature color: green

Mature color: orange

Comments: Grown in Oaxaca for use in mole sauces. Medium pungency.

▼ ▼ ▼ ▼ ▼ ▼ ▼ ▼ ▼ ▼

USDA # none

Botanical name: *Capsicum annuum* cv. 'Chilhuacle Rojo'

Common name: red chilhuacle

Location: Mexico

Seed source: collected in market; try Seed Savers Exchange

Pod length: 3 in.

Pod width: 2 in.

Immature color: green

Mature color: dark red

Comments: There is also a chilhuacle negro, which dries to a nearly black color. Used in mole sauces. Medium pungency.

▼ ▼ ▼ ▼ ▼ ▼ ▼ ▼ ▼ ▼

USDA #176463

Botanical name: *Capsicum annuum* cv. 'Dolmalik'

Common names: ancho, poblano

Location: Turkey

Seed source: USDA

Pod length: 2.75 in.

Pod width: 1.5 in.

Immature color: green

Mature color: red

Comments: Illustrates that some Mexican types are still remarkably true when grown elsewhere. An ancho is a dried poblano. Mild pungency.

▼ ▼ ▼ ▼ ▼ ▼ ▼ ▼ ▼ ▼ ▼

USDA # none

Botanical name: *Capsicum annuum* cv. 'Ancho 101'

Common names: ancho, poblano

Location: Mexico

Seed source: Enchanted Seeds

Pod length: 3.5 in.

Pod width: 2 in.

Immature color: dark green

Mature color: red

Comments: One of the most commonly grown poblano and ancho varieties. Some pods are larger. The pods are often stuffed with cheese. Mild pungency.

▼ ▼ ▼ ▼ ▼ ▼ ▼ ▼ ▼ ▼ ▼

USDA #566810

Botanical name: *Capsicum annuum* cv. 'Ancho Mulato'

Common name: mulato

Location: Mexico

Seed source: USDA

Pod length: 4.25 in.

Pod width: 2 in.

Immature color: dark green

Mature color: very dark brown

Comments: This variety is one of the darkest when dried. Used in a variety of sauces. Mild pungency.

▼ ▼ ▼ ▼ ▼ ▼ ▼ ▼ ▼ ▼ ▼

USDA # none

Botanical name: *Capsicum annuum* cv. 'Pasilla Apaseo'

Common name: pasilla

Location: Mexico

Seed source: Enchanted Seeds

Pod length: 4.75 in.

Pod width: .75 in.

Immature color: dark green

Mature color: dark brown

Comments: The name pasilla means "little raisin," a reference to the raisiny appearance and aroma of the pods. The pods can reach ten inches in length. Mild pungency.

▼ ▼ ▼ ▼ ▼ ▼ ▼ ▼ ▼ ▼ ▼

USDA # none

Botanical name: *Capsicum annuum* cv. 'Pasilla Salvatierra'

Common name: pasilla

Location: Mexico

Seed source: Enchanted Seeds

Pod length: 2.75 in.

Pod width: 1 in.

Immature color: dark green

Mature color: brown

Comments: The pods are used in sauces such as moles. Mild pungency.

▼ ▼ ▼ ▼ ▼ ▼ ▼ ▼ ▼ ▼ ▼

USDA # none

Botanical name: *Capsicum annuum* cv. 'Pasilla de Oaxaca'

Common name: pasilla de Oaxaca

Location: Mexico

Seed source: Enchanted Seeds

Pod length: 7 in.

Pod width: 1 in.

Immature color: dark green

Mature color: brown, almost black

Comments: This variety of pasilla is smoked in Oaxaca and then used to make mole sauces. Mild pungency.

▼ ▼ ▼ ▼ ▼ ▼ ▼ ▼ ▼ ▼ ▼

USDA # none

Botanical name: *Capsicum annuum* cv. 'San Felipe'

Common names: San Felipe chile, New Mexican

Location: New Mexico

Seed source: Native Seeds/SEARCH

Pod length: 2.5 in.

Pod width: 1.25 in.

Immature color: green

Mature color: red

Comments: An early form of a New Mexican pod type from San Felipe Pueblo. Medium pungency.

▼ ▼ ▼ ▼ ▼ ▼ ▼ ▼ ▼ ▼ ▼

USDA # none

Botanical name: *Capsicum annuum* cv. 'Chimayo'

Common names: Chimayo chile, New Mexican

Location: Chimayo, New Mexico

Seed source: Enchanted Seeds

Pod length: 3.5 in.

Pod width: 1.25 in.

Immature color: green

Mature color: red

Comments: An early form of the New Mexican pod type; used mostly as dried red chile. Medium pungency.

▼ ▼ ▼ ▼ ▼ ▼ ▼ ▼ ▼ ▼ ▼

USDA # none

Botanical name: *Capsicum annuum* cv. 'Española Improved'

Common names: Española chile, New Mexican

Location: New Mexico State University

Seed source: Enchanted Seeds

Pod length: 4.5 in.

Pod width: 1.25 in.

Immature color: green

Mature color: red

Comments: Developed by NMSU from an early land race; medium pungency.

▼ ▼ ▼ ▼ ▼ ▼ ▼ ▼ ▼ ▼ ▼

USDA # none

Botanical name: *Capsicum annuum* cv. 'Rio Grande'

Common name: New Mexican chile

Location: New Mexico State University

Seed source: Enchanted Seeds

Pod length: 6 in.

Pod width: 1.5 in.

Immature color: green

Mature color: red

Comments: Grown for use as green chile; mild pungency.

▼ ▼ ▼ ▼ ▼ ▼ ▼ ▼ ▼ ▼ ▼

USDA # none

Botanical name: *Capsicum annuum* cv. 'New Mexico 6-4'

Common name: New Mexican

Location: New Mexico State University

Seed source: Enchanted Seeds

Pod length: 6 in.

Pod width: 1.75 in.

Immature color: green

Mature color: red

Comments: The most commonly grown New Mexican variety for use both as green and red chile. Mild pungency.

▼ ▼ ▼ ▼ ▼ ▼ ▼ ▼ ▼ ▼ ▼

USDA # none

Botanical name: *Capsicum annuum* cv. 'Vallero'

Common name: New Mexican

Location: northern New Mexico

Seed source: Native Seeds/SEARCH

Pod length: 4 in.

Pod width: 1.5 in.

Immature color: green

Mature colors: brown and red

Comments: An early form probably related to the pasilla. Mild pungency.

▼ ▼ ▼ ▼ ▼ ▼ ▼ ▼ ▼ ▼ ▼

USDA # none

Botanical name: *Capsicum annuum* cv. 'NuMex Sunrise'

Common name: New Mexican

Location: New Mexico State University

Seed source: Enchanted Seeds

Pod length: 7 in.

Pod width: 1.5 in.

Immature color: green

Mature color: yellow

Comments: Ornamental, for use in making colored ristras. Mild pungency.

▼ ▼ ▼ ▼ ▼ ▼ ▼ ▼ ▼ ▼ ▼

USDA # none

Botanical name: *Capsicum annuum* cv. 'NuMex Sunset'

Common name: New Mexican

Location: New Mexico State University

Seed source: Enchanted Seeds

Pod length: 7.5 in.

Pod width: 1.5 in.

Immature color: green

Mature color: orange

Comments: Ornamental, for use in making ristras. Mild pungency.

▼ ▼ ▼ ▼ ▼ ▼ ▼ ▼ ▼ ▼ ▼

USDA # none

Botanical name: *Capsicum annuum* cv. 'NuMex Eclipse'

Common name: New Mexican

Location: New Mexico State University

Seed source: Enchanted Seeds

Pod length: 6.5 in.

Pod width: 2 in.

Immature color: green

Mature color: brown

Comments: Another ornamental variety for making ristras. Mild pungency. Makes excellent rellenos.

▼ ▼ ▼ ▼ ▼ ▼ ▼ ▼ ▼ ▼ ▼

USDA # none

Botanical name: *Capsicum annuum* cv. 'NuMex Big Jim'

Common names: Big Jim, New Mexican

Location: New Mexico State University

Seed source: Enchanted Seeds

Pod length: 8 in.

Pod width: 2.5 in.

Immature color: green

Mature color: red

Comments: The largest New Mexican pod type, great for home gardens. The pods are variable in form and have been known to reach twelve inches. Mild pungency. This pepper is in the *Guiness Book of World Records* as the world's largest.

▼ ▼ ▼ ▼ ▼ ▼ ▼ ▼ ▼ ▼ ▼

USDA # none

Botanical name: *Capsicum annuum* cv. 'Barker's Hot'

Common names: Barker's, New Mexican

Location: Rio Grande Valley, New Mexico

Seed source: Enchanted Seeds

Pod length: 7 in.

Pod width: 2 in.

Immature color: green

Mature color: red

Comments: This is a popular variety for green chile, particularly in the Albuquerque area. Medium pungency.

▼ ▼ ▼ ▼ ▼ ▼ ▼ ▼ ▼ ▼

USDA # none

Botanical name: *Capsicum annuum* cv. 'NuMex Sweet'

Common name: New Mexican paprika

Location: New Mexico State University

Seed source: Enchanted Seeds

Pod length: 6.5 in.

Pod width: 1.75 in.

Immature color: green

Mature color: red

Comments: Used for U.S. paprika production; nonpungent.

▼ ▼ ▼ ▼ ▼ ▼ ▼ ▼ ▼ ▼

USDA # none

Botanical name: *Capsicum annuum* cv. 'CalWonder'

Common name: bell

Location: USA

Seed source: Enchanted Seeds

Pod length: 3 in.

Pod width: 2.75 in.

Immature color: green

Mature color: red

Comments: One of the earliest bell varieties, introduced in 1828. Nonpungent.

▼ ▼ ▼ ▼ ▼ ▼ ▼ ▼ ▼ ▼ ▼

USDA # none

Botanical name: *Capsicum annuum* cv. 'Golden Bell'

Common name: bell

Location: USA

Seed source: Enchanted Seeds

Pod length: 3 in.

Pod width: 2.75 in.

Immature color: light yellow

Mature color: dark yellow

Comments: A popular colored bell. Nonpungent.

▼ ▼ ▼ ▼ ▼ ▼ ▼ ▼ ▼ ▼ ▼

USDA # none

Botanical name: *Capsicum annuum* cv. 'Oriole'

Common name: bell

Location: USA

Seed source: Stokes

Pod length: 3.75 in.

Pod width: 3 in.

Immature color: green

Mature color: orange

Comments: Nonpungent.

▼ ▼ ▼ ▼ ▼ ▼ ▼ ▼ ▼ ▼ ▼

USDA # none

Botanical name: *Capsicum annuum* cv. 'Ivory'

Common name: bell

Location: USA

Seed source: Territorial Seed Co.

Pod length: 4 in.

Pod width: 2.5 in.

Immature color: white

Mature color: yellow

Comments: Nonpungent.

▼ ▼ ▼ ▼ ▼ ▼ ▼ ▼ ▼ ▼ ▼

USDA # none

Botanical name: *Capsicum annuum* cv. 'Dove'

Common name: bell

Location: USA

Seed source: Stokes

Pod length: 3.5 in.

Pod width: 3 in.

Immature color: white

Mature color: red

Comments: Nonpungent.

▼ ▼ ▼ ▼ ▼ ▼ ▼ ▼ ▼ ▼

USDA # none

Botanical name: *Capsicum annuum* cv. 'Albino'

Common name: bell

Location: USA

Seed source: The Pepper Gal

Pod length: 2.25 in.

Pod width: 2 in.

Immature color: white

Mature color: red

Comments: Nonpungent.

▼ ▼ ▼ ▼ ▼ ▼ ▼ ▼ ▼ ▼

USDA # none

Botanical name: *Capsicum annuum* cv. 'Gold Finch'

Common name: bell

Location: USA

Seed source: Stokes Seed Co.

Pod length: 3 in.

Pod width: 2.5 in.

Immature color: ivory

Mature color: yellow

Comments: Nonpungent.

▼ ▼ ▼ ▼ ▼ ▼ ▼ ▼ ▼ ▼

USDA # none

Botanical name: *Capsicum annuum* cv. 'Duet'

Common name: bell

Location: Moldavia

Seed source: VCRI

Pod length: 3 in.

Pod width: 2.5 in.

Immature color: white

Mature color: red

Comments: Nonpungent.

▼ ▼ ▼ ▼ ▼ ▼ ▼ ▼ ▼ ▼

USDA # none

Botanical name: *Capsicum annuum* cv. 'Blondy'

Common name: bell

Location: Netherlands

Seed source: Sluis & Groot

Pod length: 2.25 in.

Pod width: 2 in.

Immature color: yellow

Mature color: red

Comments: Nonpungent. Grown in greenhouses.

▼ ▼ ▼ ▼ ▼ ▼ ▼ ▼ ▼ ▼ ▼

USDA # none

Botanical name: *Capsicum annuum* cv. 'Lilac Belle'

Common name: bell

Location: USA

Seed source: Shepherd's Garden Seeds

Pod length: 3.5 in.

Pod width: 2.5 in.

Immature color: lilac

Mature color: red

Comments: nonpungent.

▼ ▼ ▼ ▼ ▼ ▼ ▼ ▼ ▼ ▼ ▼

USDA # none

Botanical name: *Capsicum annuum* cv. 'Mexi-Bell'

Common name: bell

Location: USA

Seed source: Enchanted Seeds

Pod length: 2.75 in.

Pod width: 2.75 in.

Immature color: green

Mature color: red

Comments: This is mildly pungent bell.

▼ ▼ ▼ ▼ ▼ ▼ ▼ ▼ ▼ ▼ ▼

USDA #289762

Botanical name: *Capsicum annuum* cv. 'Idabelle'

Common name: bell

Location: Idaho, USA

Seed source: USDA

Pod length: 3.5 in.

Pod width: 4 in.

Immature color: green

Mature color: red

Comments: Bred for nematode resistance; nonpungent.

▼ ▼ ▼ ▼ ▼ ▼ ▼ ▼ ▼ ▼ ▼

USDA # none

Botanical name: *Capsicum annuum* cv. 'Kandil'

Common name: bell

Location: USA

Seed source: Redwood City Seed Co.

Pod length: 3 in.

Pod width: 2 in.

Immature color: light green

Mature color: red

Comments: Its translucent fruit quality gives it the name kandil, meaning lantern. Nonpungent.

▼ ▼ ▼ ▼ ▼ ▼ ▼ ▼ ▼ ▼ ▼

USDA # none

Botanical name: *Capsicum annuum* cv. 'Apple'

Common name: bell

Location: USA

Seed source: Johnny's Selected Seeds

Pod length: 3 in.

Pod width: 2 in.

Immature color: green

Mature color: red

Comments: Supposedly apple taste. Similar to lipstick (below); nonpungent.

▼ ▼ ▼ ▼ ▼ ▼ ▼ ▼ ▼ ▼ ▼

USDA # none

Botanical name: *Capsicum annuum* cv. 'Lipstick'

Common name: bell

Location: USA

Seed source: Johnny's Selected Seeds

Pod length: 4 in.

Pod width: 2 in.

Immature color: green

Mature colors: brown, red

Comments: nonpungent.

▼ ▼ ▼ ▼ ▼ ▼ ▼ ▼ ▼ ▼

USDA # none

Botanical name: *Capsicum annuum* cv. 'Jingle Bells'

Common name: bell

Location: USA

Seed source: Territorial Seeds

Pod length: 1.25 in.

Pod width: 1.5 in.

Immature color: green

Mature color: red

Comments: Small pods best eaten when red, can be stuffed as appetizers. Nonpungent.

▼ ▼ ▼ ▼ ▼ ▼ ▼ ▼ ▼ ▼

USDA # none

Botanical name: *Capsicum annuum* cv. 'Gypsy'

Common name: European bell

Location: Europe

Seed source: Nichols Garden Nursery

Pod length: 4.5 in.

Pod width: 2 in.

Immature color: yellow

Mature color: red

Comments: European bells differ from U.S. bells in having a tapered tip.

▼ ▼ ▼ ▼ ▼ ▼ ▼ ▼ ▼ ▼ ▼

USDA #297456

Botanical name: *Capsicum annuum* cv. 'Grande'

Common name: bell

Location: Spain

Seed source: USDA

Pod length: 4.5 in.

Pod width: 3 in.

Immature color: green

Mature color: red

Comments: Nonpungent.

▼ ▼ ▼ ▼ ▼ ▼ ▼ ▼ ▼ ▼ ▼

USDA #297460

Botanical name: *Capsicum annuum*

Common name: bell

Location: Spain

Seed source: USDA

Pod length: 5 in.

Pod width: 2.75 in.

Immature color: green

Mature color: red

Comments: Nonpungent.

▼ ▼ ▼ ▼ ▼ ▼ ▼ ▼ ▼ ▼

USDA #174127

Botanical name: *Capsicum annuum*

Common name: bell

Location: Turkey

Seed source: USDA

Pod length: 2 in.

Pod width: 1.5 in.

Immature color: yellow

Mature color: red

Comments: Nonpungent.

▼ ▼ ▼ ▼ ▼ ▼ ▼ ▼ ▼ ▼

USDA #163197

Botanical name: *Capsicum annuum*

Common name: bell

Location: India

Seed source: USDA

Pod length: 2.25 in.

Pod width: 1.5 in.

Immature color: green

Mature color: red

Comments: Nonpungent.

▼ ▼ ▼ ▼ ▼ ▼ ▼ ▼ ▼ ▼ ▼

USDA #174120

Botanical name: *Capsicum annuum*

Common name: bell

Location: Turkey

Seed source: USDA

Pod length: 2.25 in.

Pod width: 1.5 in.

Immature color: green

Mature color: red

Comments: Nonpungent.

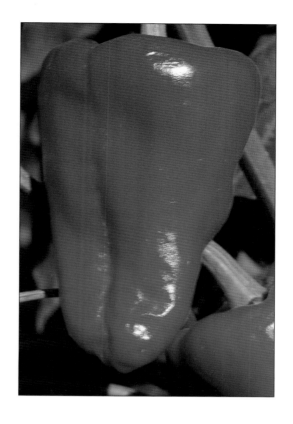

Harvesting jalapeños, Mesilla Valley, New Mexico

Afterword:
In the Land of the Chiltepíns

IT WAS LIKE A VISIT TO A BOTANICAL lost world, a chance to witness a slice of life in Mexico before the Spanish conquest. In November, at the time of the Sonoran chiltepín harvest, Dave and his wife, Mary Jane, accepted the invitation of Antonio Heras-Duran to visit the home of his mother, Josefina, the chile queen, who lives in the town of Cumpas. From there, we journeyed through the spectacular scenery of the foothills of the Sierra Madre range—chiltepín country. Our destination was the Rio Sonora valley and the villages of La Aurora and Mazocahui.

During the early days of *Chile Pepper* magazine, both of us had attended a symposium on wild chiles that was held in October, 1988, at the Desert Botanical Garden in Phoenix. The leader of the conference was the ethnobotanist Dr. Gary Nabhan, author of *Gathering the Desert*, then director of Native Seeds/SEARCH, and an expert on chiltepíns. Other chile experts attending included Dr. W. Hardy Eshbaugh, a botanist from Miami University of Ohio; Dr. Jean Andrews, author of *Peppers: The Domesticated Capsicums*; and Cindy Baker of the Chicago Botanical Garden.

As the conference progressed, we were amazed by the amount of information presented on chiltepíns. There is a wide variation in pod shapes, from tiny ones the size and shape of BBs to elongated pods a half-inch long. By contrast, domesticated piquins have much longer pods, up to three inches. The chiltepíns most prized in Mexico are spherical and measure five to eight millimeters in diameter. They are among the hottest chiles on earth, measuring up to 100,000 Scoville heat units.

The word "chiltepín" is believed to be derived from the Aztec language (Nahuatl) combination word "chilli" + "tecpintl," meaning "flea chile," an allusion to its sharp bite. That word was altered to "chiltecpin," then to the Spanish "chiltepín," and finally Anglicized to chilipiquín, as the plant is known in Texas.

In Sonora and southern Arizona, chiltepíns grow in microhabitats in the transition zone between mountain and desert, which receives as little as ten inches of rain per year. They grow beneath "nurse" trees such as mesquite, oak, and palmetto, which provide shelter from direct sunlight, heat, and frost. In the summer, there is higher humidity beneath the nurse trees, and legumes such as mesquite fix nitrogen in the soil—a perfect fertilizer for the chiltepíns. They also protect the plant from grazing by cattle, sheep, goats, and deer. Chiltepíns planted in the open, without nurse trees, often die from the effects of direct solar radiation.

Although the chiltepín plant's average height is about four feet, there are reports of individual bushes growing ten feet tall, living twenty-five to thirty years, and having stems as big around as a man's wrist. Chiltepíns lose their leaves in cold winter weather. New growth will sprout from the base of the plant if it is frozen back.

There is quite a bit of legend and lore associated with the fiery little pods. In earlier times, the Papago natives of Arizona traditionally made annual pilgrimages into the Sierra Madre Range of Mexico to gather chiltepíns. Dr. Nabhan discovered that the Tarahumara natives of Chihuahua value the chiltepíns so much that they build stone walls around the bushes to protect them from goats. Besides spicing up food, chiltepíns are used for antilactation, the technique whereby nursing mothers put chiltepín powder on their nipples to wean babies. Chiltepíns are also an aid in childbirth—when powdered and inhaled they cause sneezing. And, of course, the hot chiles induce gustatory sweating, which cools off the body during hot weather.

In 1794, Padre Ignaz Pfeffercorn, a German Jesuit living in Sonora, described the wild chile pepper: "A kind of wild pepper which the inhabitants call *chiltipin* is found on many hills. It is placed unpulverized on the table in a salt cellar and each fancier takes as much of it as he believes he can eat. He pulverizes it with his fingers and mixes it with his food. The chiltipin is the best spice for soup, boiled peas, lentils, beans and the like. The Americans swear that it is exceedingly healthful and very good as an aid to the digestion." In fact, even today, chiltepíns are used—amazingly enough—as a treatment for acid indigestion.

Padre Pfeffercorn realized that chiltepíns are one of the few crops in the world that are harvested in the wild rather than cultivated. (Others are pine nuts, Brazil nuts, and some wild rice.) This fact has led to concern for the preservation of the chiltepín bushes because the harvesters often pull up entire plants or break off branches. Dr. Nabhan believes that the chiltepín population is diminishing because of overharvesting and overgrazing. In Arizona, a chiltepín reserve near Tumacacori at Rock Corral Canyon in the Coronado National Forest has been established. Native Seeds/SEARCH has been granted a special use permit from the National Forest Service to initiate permanent marking and mapping of plants, ecological studies, and a management plan proposal.

The only way to drive to the village of the dawn (La Aurora) is to ford the Rio Sonora, which was no problem for Antonio's Jeep. The first thing we noticed about the village was that nearly every house had thousands of brilliant red chiltepíns drying on white cloths in the front yard. We stopped at the modest house of veteran chiltepínero Pedro Osuna and were immediately greeted warmly and offered liquid refreshment. As Pedro measured out the chiltepíns he had collected for Antonio and Josefina, we asked him about the methods of the chiltepíneros.

He said that the Durans advanced him money so he could hire pickers and pay for expenses such as gasoline. Then he would drive the pickers to ranches where the bushes were numerous. He dropped the pickers off alongside the road, and they wandered through the rough cattle country handpicking the tiny pods. In a single day, a good picker could collect only six quarts of chiltepíns. At sunset, the pickers returned to the road, where Pedro met them. The ranchers who owned the land would later be compensated with a liter or so of pods.

Usually, the pods would be dried in the sun for about ten days. But because that technique is lengthy and often results in the pods

Pedro Osuna measures out a liter of chiltepíns in La Aurora.

collecting dust, Antonio had built a solar dryer in back of Pedro's house. Air heated by a solar collector rose up a chimney through racks, with screens holding the fresh chiltepíns—a much more efficient method. Modern technology, based upon ancient, solar-passive principles, had arrived at the village of the dawn.

Pedro said the harvest was the best in more than a decade because the better-than-average rainfall had caused the bushes to set a great many fruits. Antonio added that during the drought of 1988, chiltepíns were so rare that there was no export crop. According to Pedro, factors other than rainfall also had an influence on the harvest—specifically, birds and insects. Mockingbirds, pyrrhuloxia (Mexican cardinals), and other species readily ate the pods as they turned red, but the real damage to the entire plant was caused by grasshoppers.

The total harvest in Sonora is difficult to estimate, but at least twenty tons of dried pods are collected and sold in an average year. Some chiltepíneros have suggested that in a wet year like 1990, fifty tons might be a better estimate. The total export to the United States is estimated at more than six tons a year, and the Durans accounted for much of that. Between 1968 and 1990, the wholesale price of chiltepíns had multiplied nearly tenfold. Between 1987 and 1990, the price had nearly tripled, mostly because of the 1988 drought. Currently, chiltepíns were being sold in South Tucson in one-quarter ounce packages for $2.00, which equates to a phenomenal $128 per pound. Thus, chiltepíns are the second most expensive spice in the world, after saffron.

Why do people in the United States lust after these tiny pods? Dr. Nabhan suggests that chiltepíns remind immigrants of their northern Mexico homeland and help them reinforce their Sonoran identity. Also, they have traditional uses in Sonoran cuisine, as evidenced by the recipes we collected. In addition to spicing up Sonoran foods, they are an antioxidant and thus help preserve *carne seca*, the dried meat we call jerky.

On the drive back to Cumpas, Antonio spoke of the possiblity of growing chiltepíns commercially. He discussed some problems with cultivated chiltepín crops. In those experiments, growers had planted the chiltepíns in rows under artificial shade and had irrigated them as if they were growing jalapeños. The cultivated chiltepíns had the tendency to produce pods 50 percent larger than the wild variety, which did not seem authentic and thus were rejected by consumers. Several reasons for the occurrence of the larger pods had been advanced. There was the natural tendency of growers to select larger pods for their seed stock for the following year, which is how chiles developed from BB-sized to the large pods we have today. Also, increased water and fertilizer could enlarge the pods.

The wild plants, when cultivated, were susceptible to chile wilt, a fungal disease aggravated by too much water. In one test planting near the Rio Montezuma, the chiltepín plants were wiped out by moth caterpillars, yet a wild population just two miles away was unaffected. One possible explanation had been offered: during times of drought, chiltepíns went dormant, as did their nurse plants. However, during the drought, chiles that were cultivated in rows and irrigated stuck out like sore thumbs and attracted pests.

But Antonio believed that clever growers could eliminate those problems. He believed that the method would be to mimic nature and improve on it only slightly. He envisioned a "natural plantation," with thousands of chiltepín plants under mesquite nurse trees and watered with drip irrigation. There were plenty of friends and relatives—especially kids—to scare off birds, spread netting to defeat grasshoppers, and pick the crop. Dogs would guard the crop from unauthorized harvesters, and solar dryers would provide a clean, perfect crop. To our best knowledge, no one—not even Antonio—has perfected such a plantation, and chiltepíns today still are as wild as they ever were.

Seed Sources

THERE IS NOT, OF COURSE, a single source for all the varieties of peppers described in this book. Following is a list of companies that provide a significant number of pepper varieties. We have recommended many of these companies as seed sources in the variety listings. (Note: some seed companies do not publish their phone numbers in their catalogs.)

The largest *Capsicum* germ plasm bank

The U.S. Department of Agriculture Plant Introduction Station in Georgia holds a vast collection of the seed of more than 2,000 *Capsicum* varieties. Gardeners interested in growing unusual peppers can petition the station for a few seeds of selected varieties. The identification numbers are given in the variety listings, if we know them. Generally speaking, the more exotic varieties, often lacking common names, are the ones most likely to have USDA numbers. There is no guarantee that the station can or will supply seed for these varieties, but it's worth a try for dedicated gardeners. Be sure to send a self-addressed, stamped envelope for the return of seed. Contact: Curator, USDA-ARS Plant Introduction Station, 1109 Experiment St., Griffin, GA 30223-1797. Phone: (770) 228-7303.

Heirloom seeds

Seed Savers Exchange is dedicated to the preservation of heirloom seed varieties, including hundreds and hundreds of *Capsicum*s. They publish an annual yearbook listing available varieties, which can be ordered though individual collectors. Seed Savers Exchange, 3076 North Winn Road, Decorah, IA 52101. Phone: (319) 382-5872.

Native Seeds/SEARCH is another source for heirloom pepper varieties, mostly from the Southwest and Mexico. Native Seeds/SEARCH, 2509 N. Campbell Ave. #325, Tucson, AZ 85719.

Home gardening seed dealers

USA

Arizona

Native Seeds/SEARCH
2509 N. Campbell Ave. #325
Tucson, AZ 85719
(602) 327-9123

Westwind Seeds
2509 North Campbell #139
Tucson, AZ 85719

California

Evergreen Y.H. Enterprises
P.O. Box 17538
Anaheim, CA 92817

Hungnong Seed America, Inc.
3065 Pachecho Pass Highway
Gilroy, CA 95020

J.L. Hudson, Seedsman
Star Route 2, Box 337
La Honda, CA 94020

Redwood City Seed Co.
P.O. Box 361
Redwood City, CA 94064
(415) 325-SEED

Shepherd's Garden Seeds
6116 Highway 9
Felton, CA 95018
(408) 335-6910

Colorado

Rocky Mountain Seed Co.
P.O. Box 5204
Denver, CO 80217

Connecticutt

Sunrise Enterprises
P.O. Box 330058
West Hartford, CT 06133

Florida

Tomato Grower's Supply Co.
P.O. Box 2237
Fort Myers, FL 33902
(813) 768-1119

The Pepper Gal
P.O. Box 23006
Ft. Lauderdale, FL 33307
(305) 565-4972

Georgia

Hastings Seedsman
P.O. Box 115535
Atlanta, GA 30310
(800) 285-6580

Idaho

High Altitude Gardens
P.O. Box 4619
Ketchum, ID 83340
(800) 874-7333

Illinois

Burgess Seed & Plant Co.
905 Four Seasons Road
Bloomington, IL 61701

Iowa

Henry Field's Seed and Nursery
415 North Burnett
Shenandoah, IA 51602
(605) 665-9391

Maryland

Johnny's Selected Seeds
202 Foss Hill Rd.
Albion, ME 04910
(207) 437-4301

Pinetree Garden Seeds
Route 100
New Glouster, ME 04260
(207) 926-3400

New Mexico

Enchanted Seeds
P.O. Box 6087
Las Cruces, NM 88006
(505) 523-6058

Old Southwest Trading Co.
P.O. Box 7545
Albuquerque, NM 87194
(505) 836-0168

Plants of the Southwest
Agua Fria Rt. 6, Box 11A
Santa Fe, NM 87501
(505) 438-8888

Seeds of Change
P.O. Box 15700
Santa Fe, NM 87506-5700
(505) 438-8080

Seeds West
P.O. Box 27057
Albuquerque, NM 87125-7057
(505) 242-7474

New York

Harris Seeds
P.O. Box 22960
Rochester, NY 14692
(716) 442-0410

Stokes Seeds
P.O. Box 548
Buffalo, NY 14240-0548
(716) 695-9649

Ohio

Liberty Seed Co.
P.O. Box 806
New Philadelphia, OH 44663

Oregon

Nichols Garden Nursery
1190 North Pacific Hwy.
Albany, OR 97321-4580
(541) 928-9280

Territorial Seed Co.
P.O. Box 157
Cottage Grove, OR 97424
(503) 942-9547

Pennsylvania

W. Atlee Burpee Co.
300 Park Ave.
Warminster, PA 18974

Twilley Seed Co.
P.O. Box 65
Trevose, PA 19053
(800) 622-SEED

South Carolina

Park Seed
Cokesbury Road
Greenwood, SC 29647
(800) 845-3369

South Dakota

Gurney Seed & Nursery Co.
110 Capitol St.
Yankton, SD 57079
(605) 665-1930

Tennesee

Alfrey Seeds
P.O. Box 415
Knoxville, TN 37901

International

Australia

Kings Herb Seeds
P.O. Box 975
Penrith, New South Wales 2751
Australia

Hungary

Budakert Ltd.
1114 Budapest
Bartok Bela UT 41
Hungary

VCRI
Vegetable Crops Research Institute
1775 Budapest, Pf. 95
Hungary

The Netherlands

Sluis & Groot Seeds
Blaker 7
2678 LW De Lier
The Netherlands

New Zealand

Kings Herbs Ltd.
P.O. Box 19-084 Avondale
Auckland, New Zealand

South Africa

Hygrotech Seed (PTY) LTS
P.O. Box 912-990
0127 Silverton
South Africa

Commercial seed sources

The following suppliers offer seeds in bulk quantities.

California
PetoSeed Co.
P.O. Box 4206
Saticoy, CA 93004
(805) 647-1188
Types: bell, cherry, squash, wax, pimiento, cayenne, ornamental, jalapeño, serrano, Cuban.

Idaho
Rogers NK
P.O. Box 4188
Boise, ID 83711
Types: various multicolored bells, 'Jupiter Bell,' jalapeños.

New Mexico
Bailey Seeds, Inc.
P.O. Box 6087
Las Cruces, NM 88006
(505) 233-3033
Types: New Mexican, ornamental, jalapeño, mirasol, pasilla, cherry, bell, habanero, rocoto, tabasco, ají, cayenne, serrano.

Ohio
Liberty Seed Co.
P.O. Box 806
New Philadelphia, OH 44663
Types: bell, Cuban, jalapeño, cayenne, wax, ornamentals.

Additional Reading

Andrews, Jean. *Peppers: The Domesticated Capsicums, New Edition.* Austin, TX: University of Texas Press, 1995.

DeWitt, Dave, and Paul W. Bosland. *The Pepper Garden.* Berkeley, CA: Ten Speed Press, 1993.

DeWitt, Dave, and Nancy Gerlach. *The Whole Chile Pepper Book.* Boston: Little, Brown, 1990.

IPGRI, AVRDC and CATIE. *Descriptors for Capsicum.* Rome: International Plant Genetic Resources Institute; Taipei, Taiwan: Asian Vegetable Research Development Center; Turrialba, Costa Rica: Centro Agronómico Tropical de Investigación y Enseñanza, 1995.

Miller, Mark. *The Great Chile Book.* Berkeley, CA: Ten Speed Press, 1991.

Naj, Amal. *Peppers: A Story of Hot Pursuits.* New York: Knopf, 1992.

Seed Savers Exchange. *Seed Savers 1995 Yearbook.* Decorah, IA: Seed Savers Exchange, 1995.

METRIC CONVERSION CHART

Inches	Centimeters	Inches	Centimeters
.25	.09	6.75	2.61
.5	.18	7	2.73
.75	.27	7.25	2.82
1	.39	7.5	2.91
1.25	.48	7.75	3
1.5	.57	8	3.12
1.75	.66	8.25	3.21
2	.78	8.5	3.3
2.25	.87	8.75	3.39
2.5	.96	9	3.51
2.75	1.05	9.25	3.6
3	1.17	9.5	3.69
3.25	1.26	9.75	3.78
3.5	1.35	10	3.9
3.75	1.44		
4	1.56		
4.25	1.65		
4.5	1.74		
4.75	1.83		
5	1.95		
5.25	2.04		
5.5	2.13		
5.75	2.22		
6	2.34		
6.25	2.43		
6.5	2.52		

Index